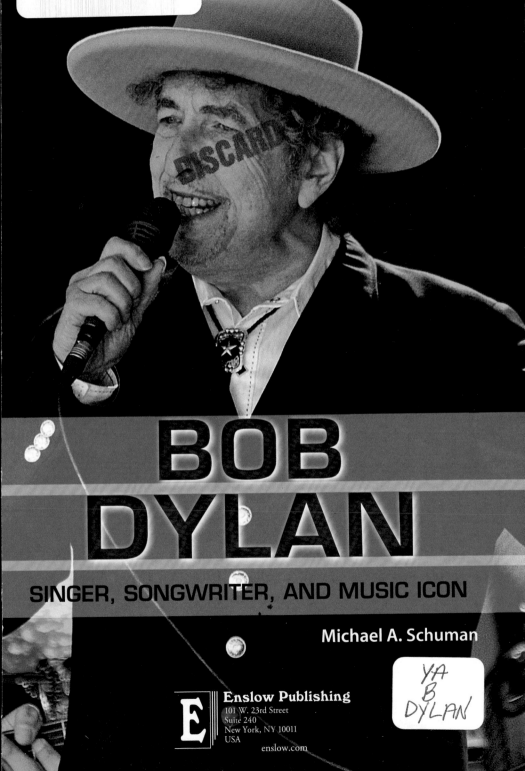

INFLUENTIAL
L!VES

BOB DYLAN

SINGER, SONGWRITER, AND MUSIC ICON

Michael A. Schuman

Enslow Publishing
101 W. 23rd Street
Suite 240
New York, NY 10011
USA

enslow.com

Published in 2019 by Enslow Publishing, LLC.
101 W. 23rd Street, Suite 240, New York, NY 10011

Library of Congress Cataloging-in-Publication Data

Names: Schuman, Michael author.
Title: Bob Dylan / Michael A. Schuman.
Description: New York : Enslow Publishing, 2019. | Series: Influential lives | Includes bibliographical references and index. | Audience: Grades 7-12.
Identifiers: LCCN 2017021491 | ISBN 9780766092068 (library bound) | ISBN 9781978501744 (paperback)
Subjects: LCSH: Dylan, Bob, 1941—Juvenile literature. | Rock musicians—United States—Biography—Juvenile literature.
Classification: LCC ML3930.D97 S33 2018 | DDC 782.42164092 [B] —dc23
LC record available at https://lccn.loc.gov/2017021491

Printed in the United States of America

To Our Readers: We have done our best to make sure all websites in this book were active and appropriate when we went to press. However, the author and the publisher have no control over and assume no liability for the material available on those websites or on any websites they may link to. Any comments or suggestions can be sent by e-mail to customerservice@enslow.com.

Portions of this book originally appeared in the book *Bob Dylan: The Life and Times of an American Icon.*

Photo credits: Cover, p. 1 Gus Stewart/Redferns/Getty Images; pp. 4, 53, 95 © AP Images; p. 9 Stephen Maturen/AFP/Getty Images; pp. 15, 19, 36, 44, 55 Michael Ochs Archives/Getty Images; p. 24 ZUMA Press Inc/Alamy Stock Photo; p. 29 Sam Falk/Archive Photos/Getty Images; pp. 33, 76 Bettmann/Getty Images; p. 40 CBW/Alamy Stock Photo; p. 46 National Archives/Hulton Archive/Getty Images; p. 57 Alice Ochs/Michael Ochs Archives/Getty Images; p. 64 Mirrorpix/Getty Images; p. 67 © Elliott Landy/The Image Works; p. 69 Cummings Archives/Redferns/Getty Images; p. 72 MGM Studios/Moviepix/Getty Images; p. 82 Keystone-France/Gamma-Keystone/Getty Images; p. 87 Jean-Louis Atlan/Sygma/Getty Images; p. 89 Ebet Roberts/Redferns/Getty Images; p. 92 Pictorial Press Ltd/Alamy Stock Photo; p. 103 AFP/Getty Images; back cover and interior pages background graphic zffoto/Shutterstock.com.

Contents

Introduction

· · · · · · · · · · · · · · · ·

When one thinks of the greatest award a person might win, their mind usually goes to a Most Valuable Player (MVP) award in sports. Or they might think of entertainment awards such as Oscars and Grammies.

However, in the eyes of most of the rest of the world, Nobel Prizes are the highest of all honors. They might not seem as glamorous as MVPs and Oscars, but the people who win Nobel Prizes are among the most respected in the world. Anyone in the world is eligible, and prizes are awarded in the categories of chemistry, medicine, peace, and literature. Among those who have won Nobel Prizes for literature are such literary heavyweights as Ernest Hemingway, William Faulkner, Samuel Beckett, and John Steinbeck.

Throughout his long career, Bob Dylan has received many awards. Still, much of the world was stunned when he won the 2016 Nobel Prize for Literature.

The world was shocked in 2016 when the Nobel Prize for Literature went to Bob Dylan. It was the first time a musician had won that honor. Even if one thought highly of Dylan's lyrics—and it's true he was considered a poet of sorts—the idea of a songwriter-musician winning the Nobel Prize for Literature seemed like blasphemy to some.

Sara Danius, the permanent secretary of the Swedish Academy, the organization that presents the Nobel Prize, defended the decision, proclaiming that Dylan "is a great poet in the English-speaking tradition."[1] Danius explained that ancient Greeks such as Homer and Sappho, "wrote poetic texts that were meant to be listened to, that were meant to be performed, often with instruments—and it's the same way with Bob Dylan."[2]

Dylan's Nobel Prize led to many discussions from people in the arts. Despite what Sara Danius said, fellow artists, musicians, and writers asked if musical lyrics can be considered true literature. A common response was, in art there is no reason why lines cannot be crossed.

American poet Billy Collins supported the decision. He declared, "Most song lyrics don't really hold up without the music, and they aren't supposed to. Bob Dylan is in the two percent club of songwriters whose lyrics are interesting on the page without the harmonica and the guitar and his very distinctive voice. I think he does qualify as poetry."[3]

And what was Bob Dylan's reaction to the great honor? Nobody knew at first. Most Nobel Prize winners comment to the media as soon as they hear the news, but Dylan has always been known for playing by his own rules. Despite the fact that Dylan is a public performer, he is a very private person. He is well known for not liking to talk to the media. Dylan didn't respond to the news until a couple of weeks after it was announced.

Late in October, rock music critic Edna Gunderson asked Dylan for his reaction. He casually responded, "Isn't that something?"[4] He added, "It's hard to believe" and it is "amazing, incredible. Whoever dreams about something like that?"[5]

The next big question was whether Dylan would travel to Stockholm, Sweden, to accept the honor in person. He first said he would, if it was possible. But in mid-November, he sent a letter to the Swedish Academy, announcing he couldn't make it because of pre-existing obligations. However, he did write a very touching speech, which was read at the Nobel Banquet by United States ambassador to Sweden Azita Raji.

Part of the speech read, "I was out on the road when I received this surprising news, and it took me more than a few minutes to properly process it. I began to think about William Shakespeare, the great literary figure. I would reckon he thought of himself as a dramatist. The thought that he was writing literature couldn't have entered his head."[6]

From the time he burst on the folk scene in the 1960s Bob Dylan was heralded as a wholly original voice for a changing America. His willingness to follow his conscience and to push his own artistic boundaries have left an indelible impression on generations of music fans, critics, and lovers of literature alike.

Radio Stations from Far Away

· ·

Bob Dylan was born on May 24, 1941, in Duluth, Minnesota, a busy port city on Lake Superior, the largest of the five Great Lakes. He was born in a local hospital and spent his earliest years in a modest two-family house on a small hillside just a few blocks from the lake. His name at birth was Robert Allen Zimmerman.

Today, Duluth is a city of about 85,000 people, but when Dylan was born the population was closer to 100,000. Lake Superior dominates the city landscape. In fact, one can easily see the giant of a lake very easily from Bob's boyhood home. Many in Duluth made their livings in jobs relating to the shipping business. Others worked in iron mines of the nearby eastern Mesabi Range. The region was so well known for its iron ranges that the people there were known as rangers.

Dylan's father, Abram Zimmerman, worked for the Standard Oil Company. Abram was a serious and practical man. He joined Standard Oil as a messenger at sixteen and worked his way up to the position of junior supervisor.

Abe's wife, Beatrice, nicknamed Beatty, liked to keep busy. If she was not working a part-time job like selling clothes in a department store, she could often be found volunteering at the local chapter of Hadassah, an organization promoting good will and education among Jews.

Bobby Zimmerman—future music superstar Bob Dylan—lived in this house in Duluth, Minnesota, until he was seven years old. The house sits on a hill overlooking the mighty Lake Superior.

The Zimmermans were practicing Jews in a place where there was not a large Jewish population. Most residents of Duluth were Lutherans of Scandinavian ancestry. There was also a sizable number of Catholics with eastern European roots. Still, there were enough Jews to support four synagogues, and according to a local historian named Joseph Papo, there was no open bigotry toward Jews.[1]

Even as a toddler, Bobby liked to sing for people. When he was three, his father took him to work, where the curly-haired child stood atop his father's desk and sang into a recording machine called a Dictaphone. A group of Abe's fellow employees gathered around, listened, and applauded when the boy finished his song.

Mother's Day Performance

A little over a year later, Bobby gave a public performance at a Mother's Day celebration in town. At first, the gathered crowd seemed uninterested. So Bobby stamped his foot on the stage and called out, "If everybody in this room will keep quiet, I will sing for my grandmother. I'm going to sing 'Some Sunday Morning.'"[2]

> "If everybody in this room will keep quiet, I will sing for my grandmother."

His mother, Beatty, recalled, "Well, he sang it, and they [the audience] tore the place apart. They clapped so hard that he sang his other big number, [a then popular show tune called] 'Accentuate the Positive.' He didn't know much more than those two songs. Our phone never stopped ringing with people congratulating me."[3]

The Zimmermans did not stay long in Duluth. After World War II ended in late summer of 1945, the mining and shipping businesses slowed down. Abe was soon laid off at Standard Oil. The Zimmermans had another mouth to feed as Bobby's brother, David Benjamin Zimmerman, was born in February 1946. In addition, Abe suffered from a disability, which made it hard to find work.

Hibbing: The City That Moved

Bob Dylan's hometown of Hibbing was founded in 1887 by a German-born businessman named Frank Hibbing. He had come to the United States with hopes of finding success in what he saw as a land of opportunity. Hibbing worked in forestry and real estate before hitting it rich in iron ore mining. Following Frank Hibbing's lead, other businesses went there to seek prosperity in the mining business. One of the bigger businesses was the Oliver Mining Company. It was discovered about one hundred years ago that the city was sitting on an incredibly fertile bed of iron ore. The Oliver Mining Company made an agreement with community leaders to relocate the entire city two miles (3.2 kilometers) south. And, quite literally, the city was rebuilt two miles away. In return, the business funded the construction of many of Hibbing's handsome civic structures that still stand today.

Years later, Bob said, "My father was a very active man, but he was stricken very early by an attack of polio [an illness causing the loss of use of one's muscles]. The illness put an end to all his dreams, I believe. He could barely walk. When we moved from the north of the country two of his brothers who were electrical fitters opened a shop and they took him with them so he could mind the shop."[4]

The shop was about 70 miles (112 km) east of Duluth in the mining town of Hibbing, Minnesota, where Abe and Beatty had lived years earlier. Being smaller than Duluth, Hibbing also had fewer Jews. But Beatty said they were friendly with the Catholics and Lutherans who lived in Hibbing and interacted together.

The Zimmerman family moved into an apartment next to Alice School, where Bob attended first grade. Bob found his first day confusing. When the bell rang for recess, he thought it meant the school day had ended, so he went home. Once he learned how long the school day was, he settled in with no problem.

A New Home

Within a year, Bob's family moved into a handsome stucco single-family house at the corner of Seventh Avenue and Twenty-Fifth Street. Abe kept busy at the shop while Beatty took a part-time job in a department store. Often Bobby's parents were not home when he returned from school, so he would head straight to his bedroom and listen to his radio or record player. He had a huge collection of small records known as 45s, short for 45 rpm, because they spin at forty-five revolutions per minute. Unlike compact discs and record albums, 45s had only one song on each side. They were more popular then than albums, and kids collected them to hear their favorite songs without having to wait for them to be played on the radio.

When he was about ten, Bobby wrote a lengthy and creative poem for Beatty for Mother's Day. The last stanza went:

My dear mother, I hope that you
Will never grow old and gray,
So that all the people in the world will say:
'Hello, young lady, Happy Mother's Day.'
Love, Bobby[5]

The next month he wrote a similar poem for his father, which ended:

I'm very lucky to have a dad this good
And if all the other kids only could,
You just can't beat him at any cost.
And without my dad, I'd be very lost.
Happy Father's Day. Love Bobby."[6]

At age twelve, Bob began lessons for his bar mitzvah, a ceremony marking the reaching of the age when a Jewish boy is responsible enough to observe God's commandments. Jewish girls have a similar ceremony called a bat mitzvah. Occurring when boys and girls turn thirteen, a bar or bat mitzvah is a very important event, usually including a long religious service followed by a party.

When the big day came, Bob, then thirteen, stood at the altar and chanted the same Hebrew prayers that

Jews have been saying for thousands of years. Between his rabbi's instruction and Bobby's talent, guests agreed the youngster did a superb job. After the religious service, around four hundred friends and relatives of the Zimmermans capped off the day by attending a gala party in the ballroom of one of Hibbing's finest hotels.

It was not always like Bob to be the center of attention. In school he was quiet and never had much to say. At home he spent time making up tunes on the family piano or writing poetry and drawing pictures alone in his bedroom. Although he had a few close friends, he felt he had different interests than most kids his age.

Early Influences

He never tired of listening to the radio. The biggest station in Hibbing, WMFG, played mainstream pop music, but Bobby found much of it boring.

At night, when many smaller stations went off the air, Bobby was able to pick up radio stations from cities and towns hundreds of miles away in the lower Mississippi River Valley. They played country music, which at the time was called country and western. Bobby's favorite country singer was Hank Williams, one of the greatest of all time. Williams told stories in his songs about heartache and lost love with titles such as "I'm So Lonesome I Could Cry" and "Your Cheating Heart." Bobby was intrigued at how Williams could emit strong feelings of loneliness in his songs.

But Williams led a short and tragic life. He fought an alcohol addiction that began when he was a teenager

Hank Williams, one of young Bob Zimmerman's favorites, is a country music legend. Williams is one of just a handful of musicians enshrined in both the Rock and Roll Hall of Fame and the Country Music Hall of Fame.

and died of an alcohol-related heart attack on New Year's Day, 1953. He was just twenty-nine years old.

Along with Hank Williams, Dylan was very impressed by a popular singer named Johnny Ray. Like Williams, Ray sang about broken hearts and unanswered love. Two of Ray's best-known songs were "Cry" and "The Little White Cloud That Cried." Ray put so much emotion into his songs that some fans said his music brought them to tears. People who did not know that he was white heard his soul-stirring delivery and thought he must be African American. Dylan said Johnny Ray was "the first singer whose voice and style I totally fell in love with."[7]

In addition to music, Bobby loved movies. His grandfather and uncle owned two of Hibbing's biggest theaters, and every week Bobby would lose himself in the fantasy world of the movie screen.

One film in 1955 caught Bobby's attention. It was titled *Rebel Without a Cause*, starring a young actor named James Dean who played a troubled teenager. Unlike many similar movies, this one portrayed Dean's character, Jimmy Stark, sympathetically. Two other teen characters were treated similarly. Their parents meant well but were out of touch and unable to help their kids. The three main characters felt alienated from their fellow teens as much as from their parents.

Bobby saw a lot of himself in Jimmy Stark. Bobby's parents tried their best but did not seem to understand the budding artist Bobby was becoming. Bobby was so taken by James Dean's character that he started dressing like him. Almost overnight, he shunned the dressy school clothes his mother had picked out for him and bought for himself some Levis, a motorcycle jacket, and a pair of biker boots.

A New Type of Music

In 1955, rock and roll was a new type of music starting to catch on among young people. Hibbing's WMFG radio station would not play it, but at night Bobby's radio picked up powerful stations from Louisiana and Arkansas playing a style of music called rhythm and blues. It was a combination of traditional African American blues and jazz with a strong backbeat, and at first it was performed almost entirely by African American musicians and singers. White artists such as

Hibbing High School

One of Oliver Mining Company's legacies to the city is Hibbing High School, built in 1920 in the shape of a capital "E." Its auditorium, with Czech crystal chandeliers, Belgian brass, and an orchestra pit is as impressive as many professional theaters. Dylan told a journalist that one of the biggest influences in his young life was a 60-foot-long (18-meter) mural gracing a wall of the high school library. It was painted by a Minnesota artist named David Tice Workman and depicts the conversion of raw iron ore into steel. One sees a steam shovel and a steam engine, but the emotional heart of the mural is the sixteen human figures representing some of the many forty nationalities that settled there to work the mines.

Pat Boone and Georgia Gibbs recorded softer, watered-down versions of the same songs.

Some white teens including Bobby liked the rougher, louder, and more soulful original rhythm and blues renditions. One of his favorite artists was Little Richard, a flamboyant African American pianist and singer from Macon, Georgia, originally named Richard Penniman. Little Richard sang and screamed his songs, known for raucous rhythms, hot piano, untamed saxophone solos, and lyrics filled with sexual undertones.

One of Bobby's friends, John Bucklin, remembered Bobby's first impression of this music. Bucklin related, "He couldn't believe it. The two of us were so hungry for anything, it didn't matter what it was, and then this sound comes along and sweeps us off our feet. We knew we were onto something that nobody else in Hibbing had any idea about—something very special—even though, at the time, we still weren't sure what it all meant."[8]

Bob tried to find ways to further explore rhythm and blues. It was not easy in mainly white Hibbing. Bob learned that in a nearby town called Virginia lived an African American disc jockey named James Reese, who played rhythm and blues music for a small private radio station. Bobby became friends with Reese, and the disc jockey taught Bobby much about rhythm and blues.

Bob decided this music would become his life's work. With three other teens, he organized a rock-and-roll band called the Golden Chords. With Bob on piano, they practiced hard and planned to show off their musical abilities at a high school talent show in March 1958. Almost the entire student body of roughly 1,500

In this still from the 1957 movie *Mr. Rock and Roll*, rock music pioneer Little Richard performs on the piano. Little Richard was one of Bob's music idols, and the teenager even tried emulating the musician's unique vocal styling.

• •

students, along with the faculty, was on hand. Student performers included a magic act, a pantomime artist, and classical musicians.

Then it was time for the Golden Chords. The band played rock-and-roll music so loud it was a wonder the school building did not shake. The audience found it hard to believe that shy, quiet Bobby Zimmerman was singing like Little Richard. Indeed, many had never heard of Little Richard and thought Bob was acting like a crazy person. Some of the students laughed at the music and thought the band looked silly. Others reveled in the new jarring sound.

One thing was for sure—Bobby Zimmerman was no longer viewed as the bashful kid who never spoke in class. He was the reigning rock and roller of Hibbing, Minnesota.

The Golden Chords did not win the talent show. The pantomime artist did. The teachers and school staff decided the music was too loud for Hibbing High School and banned rock and roll from future talent shows.

CHAPTER TWO

Next Stop Greenwich Village

• •

When Bob wasn't playing music or studying, he likely would have been in the company of a willowy blonde named Echo Helstrom. Bob had dated several girls from Hibbing High School, including a classmate named Judy Rubin. Judy and Bob got to know each other very well outside of school, too. They spent several summers together at Camp Herzl, a Jewish overnight camp in Wisconsin.

But Echo was very different from Judy. She was not Jewish and she was from a poor family. Her differences seemed to make her more attractive to him. Bob's brother David said, "Bobby always went with the daughters of miners, farmers, and workers in Hibbing. He just found them a lot more interesting."[1]

Bob and Echo enjoyed each other's company. One of their favorite activities was meeting after school and walking to a small restaurant called the L&B

Luncheonette, where they listened to their favorite songs on the jukebox and talked.

Like Jimmy Stark in *Rebel Without a Cause*, Bob was rebelling against his family's middle-class background and values. By the late 1950s, Hibbing's iron ore supply had been nearly depleted and the town's mines were laying off workers. Out-of-work miners had trouble paying their bills. Meanwhile, the Zimmerman brothers bought the store they had previously only worked at. They expanded into a larger space and began selling furniture as well as appliances. It became known as Zimmerman Electric and Furniture.

> "Bobby always went with the daughters of miners, farmers, and workers in Hibbing."

When people could not pay for the items they bought, the furniture or appliances had to be repossessed, or taken back by the store. According to service manager Benny Orlando, the Zimmerman brothers were very patient with people who could not pay their bills. He said, "The Zimmermans really leaned over backwards for a lot of people, they let it go right to the end."[2] But Bob looked down on his father for repossessing the belongings of out-of-work people. He felt his father lacked compassion for his customers who were down on their luck.[3]

Abe never held his son's feelings against him. He bought Bob a used car, then a Harley-Davidson motorcycle. When not on his motorcycle or in school,

Bob was often found playing with the Golden Chords. They rehearsed regularly on Sunday afternoons in a restaurant named Collier's, and Hibbing's teenagers stopped by to hear them play songs made famous by rock pioneers such as Little Richard, Buddy Holly, Elvis Presley, and Gene Vincent. In time, Bob tired of piano and wanted to play a portable instrument. He took lessons from the Golden Chords' guitarist Monte Edwardson and picked up the guitar quickly.

St. Paul

In June 1959, Bob graduated high school. Listed underneath his senior picture in the school yearbook were his activities: Latin Club in his sophomore year, Social Studies Club in his senior year. His ambition, the yearbook editors wrote, was "To join Little Richard."[4]

Hooking up with one of his idols might have been his dream, but Bob's immediate plans were not so exciting.

A Brush with Tragedy

One afternoon in Hibbing, Bob and a friend named Leroy Hoikkala were riding their motorcycles along nearby tracks when they stopped to let a freight train pass. Just after the train went by, Bob took off, not realizing that another train was charging down the tracks from the opposite direction. There was no time to stop, but Bob skidded out of control and overturned his bike just past the tracks, less than a foot from the charging train. Amazingly, he survived without injury.

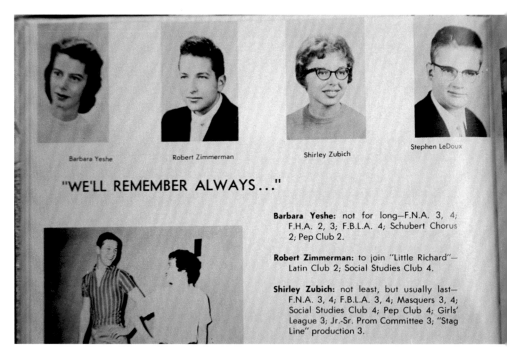

Barbara Yeshe · Robert Zimmerman · Shirley Zubich · Stephen LeDoux

"WE'LL REMEMBER ALWAYS..."

Barbara Yeshe: not for long—F.N.A. 3, 4; F.H.A. 2, 3; F.B.L.A. 4; Schubert Chorus 2; Pep Club 2.

Robert Zimmerman: to join "Little Richard"— Latin Club 2; Social Studies Club 4.

Shirley Zubich: not least, but usually last— F.N.A. 3, 4; F.B.L.A. 3, 4; Masquers 3, 4; Social Studies Club 4; Pep Club 4; Girls' League 3; Jr.-Sr. Prom Committee 3; "Stag Line" production 3.

Robert Zimmerman, soon to be known as Bob Dylan, looks serious in his graduation photo in the 1959 Hibbing High School yearbook. He listed as a goal "to join 'Little Richard.'"

He split up with Echo and like many of his fellow Hibbing graduates, traveled downstate in the fall of 1959 to attend the University of Minnesota in the big city of St. Paul.

At college Bob attended freshman classes and moved into a Jewish fraternity house, Sigma Alpha Mu. Because the first letters of the three words in the fraternity's name spelled "SAM," its members were known as Sammies.

At times, Bob entertained his fraternity brothers with his piano playing. He tried to impress them by making outrageous boasts. He bragged that he had played with Little Richard and Buddy Holly. He also claimed to be Bobby Vee, a successful pop musician at the time who had several hit records. Whether they believed him is anyone's guess.

It was not long before Bob started losing interest in his classes and having less to do with his fraternity brothers. He still lived in the SAM house but spent most of his time there alone in his room, just like he had growing up at home. His fraternity brothers began avoiding him, and Bob started to cut classes.

Although Bob had left Echo back in Hibbing, he discovered that his friend Judy Rubin lived across the street in a Jewish sorority, Sigma Delta Tau. They began seeing each other regularly. Bob also started to spend time in a part of St. Paul called Dinkytown. It was an area of small nightclubs and apartments that were home to young people known as beatniks. Beatniks generally rejected their parents' values and supported liberal

Odetta

One of Bob's first influences was an African American folk singer named Odetta Holmes. Her stage name was simply Odetta. She was born in Birmingham, Alabama, but grew up in Los Angeles. Odetta was about ten years older than Dylan and was well known in folk clubs from San Francisco to New York. Odetta had a rich, throaty voice that she put to use singing protest songs, blues, and traditional African American folk tunes. Dylan often played Odetta's best-known songs such as "Mule Skinner" and "Buked and Scorned" in his shows. Odetta died in 2008 at the age of seventy-seven.

political ideas. Beatniks considered themselves hip and others square.

A Change in Musical Tastes

Bob noticed that the beatniks in Dinkytown were ignoring rock and roll. Over the previous two years, the music had changed greatly. For several reasons, many leading rock performers were out of the picture. Buddy Holly had died in an airplane crash. Little Richard quit music to become a minister. Elvis Presley was drafted into the army. The current batch of rock-and-roll stars, including Paul Anka, Frankie Avalon, and Bobby Rydell, were clean cut and anything but rebellious.

To beatniks, folk music was hip. Folk songs are like folk stories. They were orally passed from one generation to another long before they were written down. Folk had long been viewed as the music of struggling people. Modern folk music is written down but is sung and played in the style of traditional folk. That usually means a singer is accompanied only by an acoustic guitar.

Across the nation in neighborhoods like Dinkytown, coffeehouses and folk music clubs sprouted like dandelions in spring. Several were located in cellars of old buildings. The rule seemed to be the grungier the better. Bob took note of this trend. He got rid of his electric guitar and started playing a Gibson acoustic one. Before long, he was singing in the coffeehouses and clubs of Dinkytown.

Somewhere around this time he decided that Bob Zimmerman was no name for an entertainer. He chose a new name for himself: Bob Dylan. Like much of Dylan's early life, the selection of his stage name is shrouded in mystery. Most Dylan historians say he chose the name in honor of a famous Welsh poet Dylan Thomas.

Bob has flatly denied it. In one interview, he was asked if there was a link between his name and Dylan Thomas. Bob answered, "No, none at all! If I were a fan of Dylan Thomas I would have sung his poems or I would be called Bob Thomas."[5] One rock critic, Nat Hentoff, wrote that the name Dylan was close to the last name of one of his relatives who was a gambler.[6] Others have said he named himself after Matt Dillon, a character in a then-popular television Western series, *Gunsmoke*.

> "If I were a fan of Dylan Thomas I would have sung his poems or I would be called Bob Thomas.

Regardless, Bob Dylan was now the young singer/guitarist's name. He took a few gigs, or performing jobs, wherever he could. One night he might play at the Hillel House, home of a social group for Jewish students, while the next night he would perform at a Dinkytown club called the Ten O'Clock Scholar. It was not hard to get these gigs since just about anyone with a guitar and a repertoire of a few songs was allowed to play.

Judy Rubin

Often seated at a table near the front at Dylan's gigs was Judy Rubin, who would come to listen and offer encouragement. Much of the time she brought friends with her, and they would call out requests. Bob and

Judy were falling in love with each other. But Bob had a dream that Judy was hesitant to share with him. He was on the verge of dropping out of college to try to become a full-time singer and musician. Judy wanted a more traditional life without the ups and downs involved in a musician's risky career. Because of their differences, Judy and Bob broke up in 1960.

Dylan soon became friendly with a couple named Gretel Hoffman and David Whitaker. The three shared the same interests, including liberal political views, with beat poets such as Allen Ginsberg and Gregory Corso. One day, Whitaker suggested Dylan read a book called *Bound for Glory*, written by folk singer Woody Guthrie in 1943.

In the book, Guthrie tells how he traveled around the United States, hitchhiking and hopping trains. He writes glowingly of meeting good working people going through tough times and sharing the company of homeless people. Dylan was impressed with how Guthrie championed the underprivileged through his writing and music. He identified with Guthrie and wanted to sing the praises of poor and struggling people, too.[7]

Dylan realized he was not going to achieve his dream in St. Paul. Yet he knew he was not ready for big entertainment centers such as San Francisco or New York. So after halfheartedly finishing his freshman year of college, Dylan quit school and moved to a city where folk music was just starting to catch on: Denver, Colorado.

It didn't take long for Dylan to realize that Denver was not for him. He tried playing a regular gig in a restaurant in a nearby historic mining town, Central City. It was popular with tourists who did not take folk music seriously—Dylan's or anyone else's. Dylan lasted a few days, then moved back to Denver. After a falling-out with his former roommates over some records they insisted he had stolen, Dylan felt it was time to leave. He arranged a ride with a man who was driving across the country. Accounts say Dylan arrived in New York City in either late 1960 or early 1961.

As soon as Dylan arrived in the big city, he knew just where to go. The section of New York City known as Greenwich Village had long drawn artists, writers, and

Musicians were a common sight on the streets of New York City's Greenwich Village neighborhood in the early 1960s. The area drew beatniks, poets, folk singers, and other counterculture figures.

musicians. There were several clubs in Greenwich Village, most centered around bustling MacDougal Street, where beginning musicians played for almost nothing. They did not receive a paycheck from club owners. Instead, baskets were passed through the audience for any money the crowd wished to donate. Mostly, they gave little more than pocket change.

Dylan became known for putting offbeat humor in his routines, mocking widely accepted middle-class attitudes and ideas. He would subtly put down people who were not folk music fans but who came to Greenwich Village from suburbs to see singers they considered weird. Dylan was also noted for his unusual voice, which was described at different times as tinny, whiny, metallic, nasal, and twangy. One folk singer said it was like "a dog with his leg caught in barbed wire."[8]

Dylan's unconventional appearance was something else altogether. Often seen strolling around Greenwich Village wearing a long winter coat and a black corduroy hat, Dylan was said to resemble everyone from an eastern European immigrant to a character out of a Charles Dickens novel.

He opened the evening of September 26 for a more established folk act called the Greenbriar Boys. But to the readers of the September 29 edition of the *New York Times*, it appeared the young singer was the true star. The newspaper headline read, "Bob Dylan: A Distinctive Stylist." The club's feature act appeared in smaller print under the main headline. It read, "Greenbriar Boys Are Also on Bill with Bluegrass Music." The *Times* music critic Robert Shelton wrote of Dylan, "His clothes may need a bit of tailoring, but when he works his guitar, harmonica or piano and composes new songs faster than he can remember them, there is no doubt that he is bursting at the seams with talent."[9]

On October 6, 1961, Dylan was offered his first recording contract. It stated that Dylan would record on Columbia Records for the next five years. If the first record sold poorly, Columbia could drop the contract.

"Goin' t'see Woody"

....

Most people in the arts were influenced by others before them. When he was starting out, Bob Dylan's biggest influence was Woody Guthrie. And once he'd landed in New York City, he was going to do whatever he could to meet the folk legend.

Guthrie was living an hour away in Greystone Park State Hospital in Morris Plains, New Jersey. Dylan's

Gerde's Folk City

Gerde's Folk City was originally a restaurant in Greenwich Village. It reopened as a music club in January 1960. Before long, it was one of the most popular places to listen to music. And, despite the name, it wasn't just for folk music. The list of rock legends who appeared at Gerde's includes Jimi Hendrix, Johnny Cash, Janis Joplin, Steely Dan, the Byrds, and the Mamas and the Papas.

Woody Guthrie, who wrote and popularized the folk classic "This Land Is Your Land," was one of Bob Dylan's heroes. Once he'd moved to New York, Dylan often visited Guthrie in the hospital.

• • • • • • • • • • • • • • • • • • • •

once rambunctious idol was wasting away from a rare condition called Huntington's Disease, which attacked his nervous system, causing slurred speech and uncontrollable tics. Gaunt and weak, Guthrie was only forty-nine but he looked much older.

Bob desperately wanted to meet Woody Guthrie. His Greenwich Village friends said that all Dylan ever talked about was "Goin' t'see Woody."[1]

Dylan contacted the hospital and asked if he could visit Guthrie. One might have thought a folk legend

33

> "Woody likes me—he tells me to sing for him."

would have no interest in meeting an unknown fan. But Guthrie was happy to have a visitor. Perhaps Guthrie's willingness to meet the young folk singer stemmed from the fact that he had been a resident of the hospital for approximately five years. Maybe he was hungry for company, even if it was a much younger stranger. Some have said that Guthrie's openness to meet Dylan was due to his poor mental health. They report that Guthrie was so sick that he was not thinking rationally. In his condition, they say, he would have allowed anyone to visit him. However, the majority of Dylan historians disagree and say that although Guthrie's body was weak, his mind was as sharp as ever.

Washington Square Park

Washington Square Park is a spacious public place in the Greenwich Village. Its most recognizable landmark is the commanding Washington Square Arch. For decades, the park has drawn artists and writers. In the 1950s, it became an unofficial home for the members of the Beat generation. Anyone could stop by and hear impromptu jam sessions and other music by street performers. That isn't as common nowadays. A 2011 law severely limited the places in the park where performers can play.

Guthrie recognized Dylan's talent and would often ask his caretakers when "the boy" would next be visiting. Dylan was ecstatic. In a letter home, he wrote, "Woody likes me—he tells me to sing for him—he's the greatest holiest godliest one in the world."[2]

Dylan's friend Mark Spoelstra remembered about Dylan, "It was all he wanted to talk about. He'd just been to see him that first time and had a card Woody'd signed that said 'I ain't dead yet,' on it."[3]

That was not the last meeting between Guthrie and Dylan. The veteran and rookie songsters met several times and became good friends.

Back to Greenwich Village

Back in Greenwich Village, the scrawny singer in his scruffy clothes stole any opportunity he could to play for an audience. He might do afternoons at Café Wha?, then evening and night shows at similar clubs such as the Commons, the Limelight, and the Gaslight. On Sunday afternoons, he took his guitar and harmonica and sang for free in Washington Square Park. Between shows Dylan relaxed by playing chess with other up-and-coming folk singers or going to parties that often turned into huge all-night jam sessions.

Weary of playing only other people's songs, Dylan tried his hand at writing his own. One was a tribute song, titled simply, "Song to Woody." Others were humorous in nature, such as one inspired by a newspaper account of a family outing gone awry on an excursion boat on the Hudson River. Dylan titled it "Talking Bear Mountain

Before long, Bob Dylan became a regular performer at clubs around Greenwich Village. Here, he performs on an acoustic Gibson guitar onstage at Gerde's Folk City in Greenwich Village in 1961.

Picnic Massacre Blues," and it always drew laughs from assembled crowds.

The nineteen-year-old Dylan gradually became known to area

> **We made a conscious effort of being by ourselves.**

club owners and eventually was offered a real paycheck. It was at Gerde's Folk City, and Dylan debuted there on April 11, 1961. It was at Folk City that he met a pretty, dark-haired, seventeen-year-old fan named Suze (pronounced "Suzy") Rotolo. Before long, they were a couple and Suze happily followed Dylan around, sitting up front whenever he performed.

Suze and Bob appeared to be a great team. They were attracted to each other and were both dreamers. Years later Suze recalled, "We made a conscious effort of being by ourselves, shutting out the rest of the world."[4] In the nighttime, the couple hung around the coffeehouses and nightclubs of Greenwich Village.

Things were progressing nicely for Bob Dylan. It was in the fall of 1961 that Dylan made the acquaintance of a famous talent scout named John Hammond who signed him to his first record deal with Columbia Records But in the reality of the cutthroat business of the music world, Bob Dylan had a long way to go.

John Hammond
Takes a Chance

●●●●●●●●●●●●●●●●●●●●●●●●●●●

It is very difficult for virtually unknown performers to achieve fame without the assistance of publicity, and this was particularly true during the pre-Internet age. Record companies send information in the form of news releases about their performers to the media. If a reporter for a website, newspaper or magazine, or perhaps television or radio is interested in the new performer, they may want to interview the person for a story. Of course, one with a fascinating background makes for good interviews.

Bob Dylan was aware of the power of publicity and liked telling tall tales about himself. One of Dylan's earliest interviews was with Columbia Records publicist Billy James in the fall of 1961. Dylan related to James a colorful history about his life, much of it false. He admitted he was from northern Minnesota but also claimed to have run away from home. How old was he at the time, James asked. "Uh, about seven. Seven—eight—something like that," Dylan answered.[1]

Dylan laid it on thicker and heavier as the interview continued. He claimed to have traveled the country working as a carnival roustabout, or

> "Lots of songs that people are singing today I learned in that carnival."

unskilled laborer. Of his so called carnival days, Dylan told James, "I didn't sing for any money but I learned a lot of songs in the carnival. Lots of songs that people are singing today I learned in that carnival. That's why I know all these songs they do now—at least a folk song—I've heard a version of it or something like it before."[2]

This fake Dylan biography was sent to much of the media, and people had no reason to believe it was not true.

John Hammond Jr.

John Hammond Jr. was a talented musician who excelled at both piano and violin. Yet he made his career as a talent scout and music producer, not a musician. He was also from a different era than Dylan. Hammond was best known for discovering some of the greatest legends of the big band era in the 1930s and 1940s, but he showed all doubters that he could recognize talent in the folk community as well.

First Album

Dylan recorded his first album for Columbia in November 1961. It included original numbers, such as "Song to Woody," but also his versions of standard blues and folk tunes such as "Pretty Peggy-O" and "House of the Risin' Sun." Then he had to wait for Columbia to release it to radio stations and record stores.

But Columbia Records was not in a rush to release Dylan's album. Even though Columbia paid Dylan to record it, there would be greater costs to press it and ship copies. Some Columbia executives wondered whether it was wise to invest any more money in the album. Many

Bob Dylan's eponymous first album was released on March 19, 1962. Although not a commercial success, it was just the first of dozens he would record.

thought Dylan's voice was too strange for him to become successful.

In these early days of rock and roll, the majority of radio stations played hit 45s, not album cuts. Albums were viewed as collections of an artist's hit singles, with a few throwaway songs included to fill space. Columbia's director of artists and repertoire (A&R), Dave Kapralik, and other company executives felt there was not a single song on Dylan's album that had the potential to be a popular 45.

Kapralik and others thought John Hammond had made a big mistake in signing Dylan. They felt Hammond was out of touch with the young people of the early 1960s. Those at Columbia referred to Dylan as "Hammond's Folly." But Hammond was convinced Dylan had what it took to be a hit. He spoke to as many people as he could at Columbia, urging them to take a chance on this new talent. His efforts worked, and Dylan's first album was released on March 19, 1962. It was titled simply, *Bob Dylan*.

The album received some good reviews but was not a financial success. Kapralik said that was enough of a reason to drop Dylan's contract. Again, Hammond went to bat for Dylan. And again, he convinced Kapralik and other Columbia executives to keep him.

Dylan kept busy writing songs. One was a biting satire of an ultra-conservative political group called the John Birch Society. Dylan called it "Talkin' John Birch Paranoid Blues," and he used words like knives, brutally attacking the group as a bunch of closed-minded extremists.

A New Song Catches On

Another new Dylan song was "Blowin' in the Wind." It is a haunting ballad in which Dylan asks questions about freedom, war, peace, and life, and death. But he does not give answers. He sings that the answers are "blowin' in the wind."

Many of Dylan's friends loved the song. They thought it was profound and asked meaningful questions. Others were not sure. One respected folk singer named Dave Van Ronk first thought, "What an incredibly dumb song. I mean, what the hell is 'blowing in the wind?'"[3]

Abut a month and a half later, Van Ronk changed his mind. He recalled, "I was walking through Washington Square Park and heard a kid singing, 'How much wood could a woodchuck chuck if a woodchuck could chuck wood? The answer, my friend, is blowin' in the wind.'" At that point, I knew Bobby had a smash on his hands!"[4]

Dave Van Ronk

Dave Van Ronk was a big man with a gravelly voice. He played guitar and banjo and became one of the towering figures of folk music starting in the late 1950s. He not only performed outdoors in Washington Square Park and inside Greenwich Village's coffeehouses—he also let his apartment become a sort of open house for neighborhood folk musicians. He was so active in the Greenwich Village scene that the residents gave him an unofficial title: the Mayor of MacDougal Street. Van Ronk was sixty-six when he died of cancer in 2002.

Dylan's relationship with his friend Suze Rotolo provided inspiration for another song. Bob and Suze had been having arguments in which she claimed that he was controlling her. Dylan responded that she did not appreciate him. Suze split up with Dylan, leading him to write a song called "Don't Think Twice, It's Alright." Unlike his songs with political themes, "Don't Think Twice, It's Alright" was about a scorned lover telling an ex-girlfriend good-bye and good riddance.

On August 9, 1962, Dylan officially said good-bye to Bobby Zimmerman and legally changed his name to Bob Dylan. He spent much of the following spring recording his second album. Outside the studio, he was setting off fireworks with his words and actions. He was rude to the media. In an interview for an alternative New York City newspaper, the *Village Voice*, Dylan was asked whether he was influenced by Hank Williams. Dylan responded, "Hey, look, I consider Hank Williams, Captain Marvel, Marlon Brando, The Tennessee Stud, Clark Kent, Walter Cronkite and J. Carroll Naish all influences. Now what is it—please—what is it exactly you people want to know?"[5] Captain Marvel and Clark Kent are comic book characters. Walter Cronkite was a news anchor, The Tennessee Stud is a fictional horse, and J. Carroll Naish was a character actor.

Two months later, he made a decision that few up-and-coming entertainers would have the nerve to do. Dylan turned down a chance to appear on the influential variety show *The Ed Sullivan Show*, one of the most-watched television programs in its day. It would have been wonderful publicity for his second album.

Bob Dylan is photographed with girlfriend Suze Rotolo. Their breakup inspired Dylan to write one of his classic songs, "Don't Think Twice, It's All Right."

Dylan wanted to sing "Talkin' John Birch Paranoid Blues." The show's staff would not allow him to perform it. They said it was too controversial and asked him if he would play something else. He quietly responded, "No, this is what I want to do. If I can't play my song, I'd rather not appear on the show."[6]

It turned out that not appearing on the Sullivan show may have been better for Dylan's career than actually performing. Young people heard about the incident and respected him for having

"If I can't play my song, I'd rather not appear on the show."

the courage to stand up for what he believed in.

Dylan's second album, *The Freewheelin' Bob Dylan*, was released May 27, 1963. Featured on the cover was a photograph of Dylan walking side by side with Suze. The song that caused so much trouble, "Talkin' John Birch Paranoid Blues," was included on early copies but cut from later recordings. Songs that did made the album included future classics "Blowin' in the Wind" and "Don't Think Twice, It's Alright." Almost all the album cuts were written by Dylan.

Reviews

The album received rave reviews and was a major hit. It helped that a popular folk trio named Peter, Paul & Mary recorded "Blowin' in the Wind" and released it as a 45 early in the summer. The trio had just had a huge hit with a 45 called "Puff (The Magic Dragon)." "Blowin' in the Wind" was a perfect follow-up song. It peaked at number 2 on the national chart that summer. Peter, Paul & Mary followed up that hit with Dylan's "Don't Think Twice, It's Alright," which made it to number 9.[7]

"Blowin' in the Wind" was the standout song from Dylan's second album. It represented the ideas and dreams of liberal young people who wanted to make a difference in the world. Dylan sang it in late July at his first appearance at the Newport Folk Festival, an annual event in Newport, Rhode Island, showcasing the best folk performers in the world. Critics said Dylan was the hit

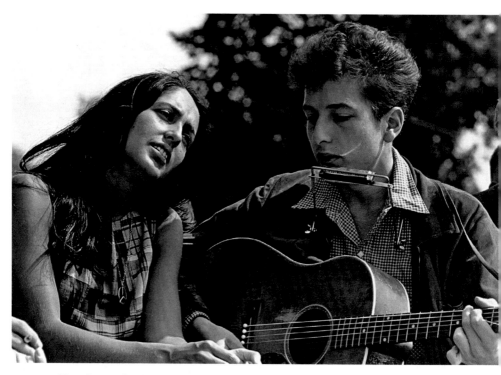

Two legends, Joan Baez and Bob Dylan, perform at the famous March on Washington for Jobs and Freedom in Washington, DC, in 1963. It was here that Martin Luther King Jr. delivered his legendary "I have a dream" speech.

of the show. In just a few months, Dylan had grown from just another singer with talent to a folk music superstar.

Suze and Bob decided to get back together that year. Meanwhile, Dylan continued to work on new songs and perform live concerts for the rest of 1963. In August, he performed at the famous March on Washington, where Dr. Martin Luther King Jr. gave his historic "I have a dream" speech.

Then on October 26, Dylan played in a place reserved for the world's most respected musicians: Carnegie Hall in New York City. Dylan flew his parents in from Minnesota for the show. They were delighted to see their son play, but some reporters said he was rude to them by ignoring them after his performance.

As he became famous, the press started researching his past. Many establishment reporters were thrilled to tell their readers that Bob Dylan was as phony as a three-dollar bill. In its November 4, 1963, issue, *Newsweek* magazine quoted Dylan saying, "I don't know my parents. They don't know me. I've lost contact with them for years."[8] In the following sentence, *Newsweek* said, "A few blocks away Mr. and Mrs. Abe Zimmerman of Hibbing, Minn. were looking forward to seeing their son sing at Carnegie Hall. Bobby had paid their way east and had sent them tickets."[9]

What a liar, *Newsweek* readers must have thought. People who did not like his style reveled in the report. But his fans did not seem to mind. That included perhaps his biggest fan at the time, a well-known folk singer named Joan Baez. She had warmly introduced Dylan at Newport, and soon they were seeing each other romantically. Dylan was still seeing Suze as well. Dylan historians have differing views on how much Suze and Joan knew about each other at that time.

Dylan's third album, *The Times They Are A-Changin'*, came out in February 1964. The title song became its best-known cut. Dylan's newfound fame was having an effect on him. On one hand, he enjoyed the attention, but only when he was in the right mood. On the other hand, he was annoyed by his sudden lack of privacy. People approached him on the street to ask for autographs and discuss political issues. Others claimed to be old friends and requested special favors. Dylan decided he needed a break.

A couple of days after the release of *The Times They Are A-Changin'*, Dylan and three friends took off on a lengthy road trip. They did not plan to stop at tourist attractions but to meet the real people of America, as Woody Guthrie had. First, they brought clothes to striking coal miners in Kentucky. They then paused in New Orleans, where Dylan encountered racial segregation firsthand. Dylan found it disturbing when an African American man they had befriended was not allowed to enter a restaurant with them.

On New Orleans's famed Bourbon Street, they joined a crowd surrounding a street musician playing "Don't Think Twice, It's Alright." Dylan told the kid he played well. When he started singing along to the man's next tune, the singer stopped suddenly, spurting out, "You! I mean. It couldn't be. No, it's impossible!" Dylan simply replied, "You sing that very well," and moved on.[10]

The road trip ended in California, where Dylan appeared on a television show and met up with Joan Baez. When Dylan returned to New York in March, Suze Rotolo confronted him. Again, she accused Dylan of controlling her. She also suspected that he and Joan Baez had gotten together in California. Dylan and Rotolo split for good.

Rotolo later said, "As Dylan got more and more famous, things got more and more oppressive. It was a whole bad time and I really crumbled. I didn't see myself as Bob Dylan's wife. All I wanted to do was get away from it all."[11]

Though finished with Suze, Dylan continued dating Joan Baez. But he also started seeing a different woman he had met several months earlier. She was an exotic, dark-haired beauty named Sara Lownds, a twenty-five-year-old divorced woman with a young daughter named Maria.

What Really Happened at the Newport Folk Festival?

· · · · · · · · · · · · · ·

Dylan might have been discovering the country in early 1964, but young people were discovering something else—an entirely new style of music. And the biggest name in the music business then was British group the Beatles.

Through the winter, spring, and into the summer of 1964, one Beatles song after another hit number one on the US charts. Some had been recorded as many as two years earlier and had already been hits in Europe. It had taken a while for the group, consisting of John Lennon, Paul McCartney, George Harrison, and Ringo Starr, to catch on in the United States. But once they did, American musical tastes would never be the same.

Rock songs replaced acoustic folk music in popularity. The sudden change in music was absolutely shocking.

Some of the most established hit-makers, such as Connie Francis, the Shirelles, Chubby Checker, and the Everly Brothers saw their careers stop dead in their tracks.

Other Sides of Dylan

How did this affect Bob Dylan? At first, not much. He still had his usual folk fanatics who tried to figure out hidden meanings in his songs and anxiously awaited every new Dylan album. At the Newport Folk Festival in July 1964, he debuted two new songs, "All I Really Want to Do" and "It Ain't Me, Babe." Both were personal numbers about friendship and love, and some in the audience were disappointed that he shied away from political material. That assignment was left to Dylan's girlfriend Joan Baez, who closed the Friday evening concert with the unofficial anthem of the civil rights movement, "We Shall Overcome."

Dylan's next album, *Another Side of Bob Dylan*, came out in August 1964 and included the two songs he premiered a month earlier in Newport. Dylan insisted the album's title was his producer's idea. Dylan later said, "I didn't want them to call [my fourth album] *Another Side of Bob Dylan* because I thought it was just too corny."[1]

It was not a colorful title, but it did make fans wonder, "What other side?" One Dylan historian explained, "The 'another side' it showed was his inside."[2] That meant that the songs were more about Dylan's feelings rather than social issues. Many critics panned the album, saying it did not have the creativity of his earlier work. Fans bought copies, but not as many as before.

Despite his success and fame, Dylan was just twenty-three years old. Most people at that age are recent college graduates just starting out in their careers. Like many people that young, Dylan was experimenting with his life, some of it unwisely. He began taking LSD. Marijuana had been part of the folk scene for some time. But LSD is a much more dangerous drug. As the 1960s progressed, drug use among musicians and other young people would spread.

Subterranean Homesick Blues

Dylan's next album, *Bringing It All Back Home,* was released in March 1965. It included both rock-influenced songs and traditional acoustic numbers. One, "Subterranean Homesick Blues," would become a Dylan classic. "Subterranean Homesick Blues" was a long way from the simple questions of "Blowin' in the Wind." It was a fast-paced number full of rapid-fire lyrics of basic rhymes, taking on everything from the education system to the government. Considering how popular Dylan was, it was amazing that he had never had a hit 45. "Subterranean Homesick Blues" was his first. It peaked at number 39 in May.[3]

Around the same time that *Bringing It All Back Home* came out, Dylan made a brief side trip into movies. A filmmaker named D. A. Pennebaker shot a documentary film of a Dylan tour in England in the spring of 1965. It was called *Don't Look Back* and was shot in a technique called *cinema verite*. There was no script. Pennebaker shot action as it happened, whether it was Dylan singing in concert or arguing with a reporter

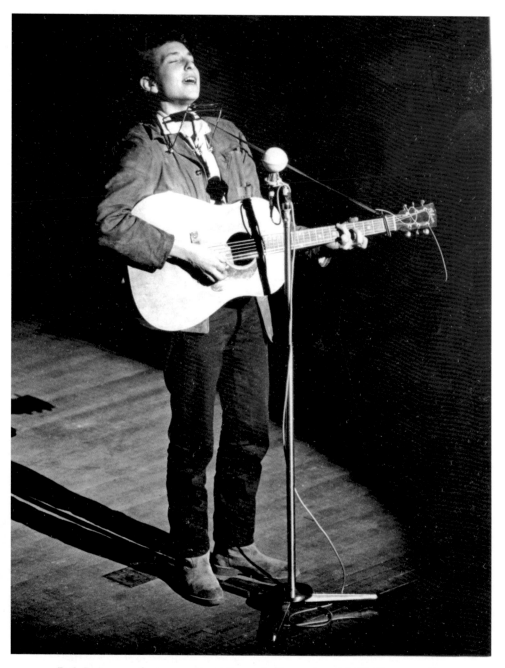

Bob Dylan performs onstage in early November 1963. Two months later he would embark on an exploratory road trip to meet a segment of the population he called the real people of America.

from *Time* magazine. It played in theaters specializing in art films. Critics were divided in their opinions. Those who liked Dylan also liked the movie. Those who were not Dylan fans blasted it. One newspaper, the *Atlanta Journal,* called it a "boring, off-color home movie of the neighborhood's biggest brat blowing his nose for 90 minutes."[4]

Of course, newspapers were never among Dylan's biggest supporters, since he continued to toy with reporters. He said to a member of the British press that year, "Actually, the first record I made was in 1935."[5] That would have been an amazing trick considering that Dylan was born in 1941.

Dylan and Sara Lownds were becoming closer as a couple. It seemed that the more he saw of Sara, the less he respected Joan Baez. Baez wrote a letter to her sister Mimi while on tour with Dylan in May 1964. In it she said, "We're leaving Bobby's entourage. He has become so unbelievably unmanageable that I can't stand to be around him."[6]

Dylan's sixth album, *Highway 61 Revisited,* was released in August 1965. It included "Like a Rolling Stone," which had been released as a 45 and peaked at number 2 that summer. Many critics have said "Like a Rolling Stone" is Dylan's best song ever. It is a rambling tune, lasting about six minutes. On the surface, it seems mean-spirited. Dylan appears to be getting pleasure from

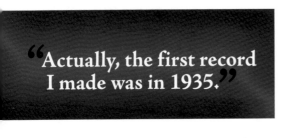

"Actually, the first record I made was in 1935."

Dylan played many other instruments besides the guitar. Here he plays the harmonica in a New York City recording studio in January 1965 while recording the album *Bringing It All Back Home.*

the troubles of an old girlfriend who once acted as if she was better than he. But like much of Dylan's words, those to "Like a Rolling Stone" can be taken on different levels. Music critic Robert Shelton says the song is "about the loss of innocence and the harshness of experience."[7]

"Like a Rolling Stone" makes prominent use of guitar, harmonica, Dylan's straining voice, and the intense organ work of keyboard player Al Kooper. It was very different from Dylan's early songs, in which he accompanied himself only by acoustic guitar.

Controversy at Newport

This was part of the new trend. Not all folk diehards accepted it, as proven by a very controversial appearance Dylan made at the 1965 Newport Folk Festival.

Over the years, his performance on that July day on the Rhode Island coast has become a folk tale in itself.

The Newport Folk Festival

In 1954, a group of jazz fans started the Newport Jazz Festival, an annual event where some of the best performers gathered in the resort community of Newport, Rhode Island, to perform for thousands of fans. Not to be outdone, in 1959 the folk community organized the Newport Folk Festival. In its first years, it showcased mainly folk music, but it soon embraced several kinds of American music, including blues, country, and indie folk. It still takes place annually, over the course of a weekend in mid-summer.

In his famous and controversial appearance at the 1965 Newport Folk Festival, Dylan abandoned his acoustic guitar and took up a Fender Stratocaster electric guitar.

• • • • • • • • • • • • • • • • • • • •

What really happened has never been clear. Even those in attendance have not agreed on what took place.

The most-told story of July 25, 1965, goes like this: Dylan came onstage sporting not his usual acoustic guitar, but an electric one and with a rock band behind him. He played three songs. The first was a pro-labor tune he wrote called "Maggie's Farm." A chorus of boos was heard from the audience.

Dylan's second and third songs were "Like A Rolling Stone" and "It Takes a Lot to Laugh, It Takes a Train to Cry." The booing did not let up. In response, Dylan left the stage. He returned with an acoustic guitar and played two folk songs in the traditional manner. The audience then accepted him, after giving him a clear message that they would not allow him to ruin folk music by cheapening it.

But what really happened? A music historian named Sam Charters studied films and recordings of Dylan's short electric set and insisted the only loud objections from audience members were about the quality of the sound system. Charters said, "There were no boos and the complaints weren't about the music—My God, Dylan was the hottest thing going. The sound system at Newport was not set up properly for electric instruments, so people were yelling out because all they could hear was noise."[8]

Dylan's organ player Al Kooper said years later that the audience booed because Dylan's music set was too short. The person at the sound console, Paul Rothchild, was in charge of controlling the loudness of Dylan's music. He recalled things a bit differently. "From my perspective, it seemed like everybody on my left wanted Dylan to get off the stage, everybody on my right wanted him to turn it up. And I did—I turned it up."[9]

Dylan was convinced the audience was booing him personally. According to Dylan, "They certainly booed, I'll tell you that. You could hear it all over the place. I was kind of stunned. But I can't put anybody down for coming and booing. After all, they paid to get in. They could have been maybe a little quieter and not so persistent, though."[10]

When Dylan came back onstage with his acoustic guitar, he sang one of his own compositions, "It's All Over Now, Baby Blue." Was he telling the audience that his period as a folk purist was all over? According to Paul Rothchild, "To me, that night at Newport was as clear as crystal. It's the end of one era and the beginning of another."[11]

Despite the fact that Dylan was now writing songs with personal as well as social messages, college students continued to hold him in high regard. In an informal survey taken at three Ivy League colleges that fall, students voted Dylan their "favorite contemporary American writer."[12] Not all students felt that way. One said "it was 'absurd' to take Dylan's writing seriously."[13]

"It's the end of one era and the beginning of another."

But enough respected his words that several music artists around this time jumped on the Dylan bandwagon. They recorded Dylan songs, which in turn became hit 45s. A Los Angeles band, the Byrds, had a number-one smash with an electrified version of "Mr. Tambourine Man."[14] Another band from Los Angeles, the Turtles, took their version of "It Ain't Me Babe" to number 8 in the fall of 1965.[15] Cher had her first solo hit with Dylan's song "All I Really Want to Do." It reached number 15 that same fall.[16] A few months later, one of rock music's finest vocal groups, the Four Seasons, recorded an up-tempo version of "Don't Think Twice" under the fake name the Wonder Who. It peaked at number 12.[17]

In homes across America, teenagers tuned their radios to local rock stations, just as young Bobby Zimmerman had in his Minnesota home ten years earlier. Instead of hearing the music of Little Richard, they were tuned into the songs of Bob Dylan. It did not matter if they were sung by Dylan or some other group. Dylan had become a full-fledged star. The question on the minds of rock fans was, "What would Bob Dylan do next?"

Major Changes

•••••••••••••••••••••••••••

D ylan and his electric guitar were still turning fans
into critics well into 1965. Whenever he brought
out the electric guitar on stage, some diehard fans booed
him. Some even yelled for him to get off the stage. At
a concert at the Forest Hills Music center in New York
City, people yelled out, "We want the old Dylan."[1] The
New York Times music critic Robert Shelton called the
audience "rude and immature," and wrote, "By the time
they [the audience] get to know his excellent new folk
rock songs, maybe the noisy young boors who ruined
an artistically strong concert may have grown up a bit."[2]

But Dylan's rock-oriented fans loved the new sound
and celebrated it by dancing in the aisles. Between the battle
of the folkies and the rockers, the rockers were winning.

Next Steps

Dylan took time off from touring to marry Sara Lownds
in the Long Island town of Mineola, New York, on

Bob Dylan's High School Reunion

Dylan returned to Hibbing, Minnesota, for his tenth high school reunion. Unfortunately, many former classmates weren't ready to welcome him home. There were several reasons for that. Local bookstore owner Mary Keyes is a Hibbing native and a Dylan expert. She occasionally leads guided tours of Hibbing locations that played important roles in Dylan's life. Keyes recalled, "They wanted him to be driven [through town] in a parade and wave to the crowd. That is a very un-Dylan-like thing to do. They resented that he fibbed about his background and didn't discuss being from Hibbing, that he left town right away. I left town right away, too. A lot of us wanted to leave here. It's a small town. And some were just probably jealous."[3] He then swore he'd never again attend a class reunion. And he never did.

November 22, 1965. The ceremony was small and so secret that he did not even tell his parents, brother, or best friends. Why Dylan remained so silent about his marriage is unknown, but it is believed that he just wanted privacy. Just about two months after the marriage, Sara gave birth to a son, Byron Dylan, on January 6, 1966. The public learned about the baby when a newspaper, the *New York Post*, discovered the news and reported it on February 9, 1966.

The question, "What would Bob Dylan do next?" was answered in May 1966, when his album titled *Blonde on Blonde* was released. It is to many Dylan critics his all-time finest album. It was also his first not recorded in New York. Dylan's then-producer Bob Johnston suggested recording the record in Nashville, Tennessee, the city known as the capital of country music. Johnston knew several Nashville musicians who could play backup.

Blonde on Blonde contained songs that have become Dylan classics. A ballad, "Just Like a Woman," is about male and female relationships. Other often-played cuts from *Blonde on Blonde* include the mournful "Stuck Inside Mobile with the Memphis Blue Again," and "I Want You," in which he pleads for a woman not to leave him.

A Rollicking Song

The most controversial and successful number was a rolling, raucous party song with a loud horn section. Its title was "Rainy Day Women #12 and 35." The words in the title appear nowhere in the song. The frequently repeated chorus goes, "Everybody must get stoned." Those who took the song at face value believed it was a drug song and that a "rainy day woman" was slang for a marijuana cigarette. The song was released as a 45 and reached number two on the national chart early in the summer of 1966.[4] That was in spite of the fact that many radio stations refused to play it.

Was the song really about drugs? Some said Dylan's use of the word "stoned" was meant to be taken literally. Stoning somebody, or hitting them with stones until they die, is a common punishment in the Bible. Dylan could have been saying that any person who takes a stand will be "stoned." That did not mean he or she would be put to

As a popular entertainer, Dylan was often the airline industry's best friend. He and his wife, Sara Lownds, are seen walking through London's Heathrow Airport.

death but be snubbed or shut out by others. When asked, Dylan simply answered that he never would write a song about drugs.

True or not, Dylan's friends noticed in the mid-1960s that Dylan was heavily using drugs. His skin had turned pale and his eyes drooped. Dylan appeared nervous and shaky. Friends said he would stay up for days without sleeping. He was not only rude to the media but to those who knew him.

At this time the Vietnam War was raging and dividing America. Rock musicians, including Dylan, and others were questioning whether the United States was right to be involved in the war. On the other side were the military and its supporters who felt it was unpatriotic to disagree with America's support of South Vietnam against communist North Vietnam. It was a heated issue and became the basis for emotional arguments in classrooms and living rooms everywhere. In addition, many rock musicians, with their grubby clothes and long hair, contrasted greatly with the clean-cut looks and spit-and-polish uniforms of the military.

But Dylan's drug addiction was apparent on the tour. He often slurred words while onstage. While riding in a limousine with John Lennon of the Beatles one night, Dylan was so ill he vomited in the back seat. Dylan returned to New York in June, sick and exhausted. He learned that his manager had booked him for sixty more concerts. In need of a break, Dylan went to the town of Woodstock, New York, where he kept a retreat. Woodstock is a country town about one hundred miles from New York City at the base of the Catskill Mountains.

Dylan and Woodstock

Curiously, Dylan did not appear at perhaps the most famous rock concert of all time, the original Woodstock, which took place not far from his home. The 1969 three-day concert featured headline bands and drew hundreds of thousands of fans. With such a major gathering so close by, why was Dylan absent? He later stated that he ignored Woodstock because he was sick of uninvited fans coming to his house day and night. "They kept comin'. This was just about the time of that Woodstock festival, which was the sum total of all this. I couldn't get any space for myself and my family, and there was no help, nowhere. I got very resentful about the whole thing, and we got outta there."[5]

Artists and writers are attracted to its beauty and small-town features, and Dylan was right at home.

The Accident

In late July 1966, Dylan cheated death again. And once more, it had to do with a motorcycle. Dylan told Robert Shelton that after being awake for three days, he was taking his bike to a repair shop. On the way, he hit an oil slick. The back wheel locked and Dylan was thrown over the handlebars. However, that is only one of many stories about what happened. Another account says that he was simply doing wheelies at

"I couldn't get any space for myself and my family."

his home and he took the spill. Regardless, it began a major change in Dylan's life.

Dylan recovered from his injuries, then for the next few years practically quit show business. He also dropped out from public sight. He reduced—and according to some people, ended—his dependency on drugs. His family was growing. A daughter, Anna, was born on July 11, 1967 followed by a son named Samuel on July 30, 1968 and another son, Jakob, on December 9, 1969.

Why did Dylan take the time off from his career? A few years later, he said, "I didn't sense the importance of that accident till at least a year after [it happened.] I

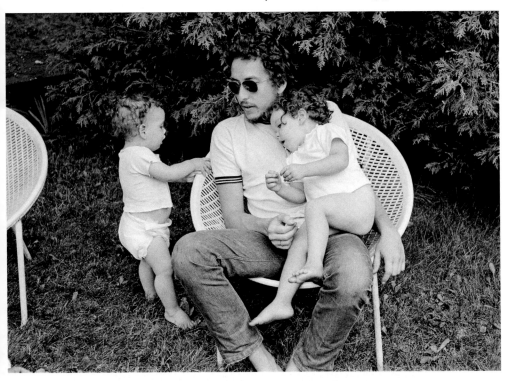

Dylan relaxes at his Woodstock, New York, home with his children Sam and Anna in the late 1960s. After so many years living in the spotlight, the musician retreated to spend time with his family.

realized that it was a real accident. I mean I thought that I was just gonna get up and go back to doing what I was doing before, but I couldn't do it anymore."[6]

The Anti-hero

Even though he quit making public appearances, Dylan did not stop writing and recording. He jammed with five backup musicians who later became a successful rock group called the Band. They played Dylan compositions, as well as folk standards in both a room in Dylan's home and in the basement of a house his backup musicians rented and nicknamed Big Pink. Once in a while they taped their music, but Dylan had no immediate intention of releasing these sessions on albums.

On the other hand, he did record albums meant to be released. One, titled *John Wesley Harding*, came out in January 1968. Except for a greatest-hits collection that came out in the spring of 1967, it was his first album since *Blonde on Blonde*. The album was named for a real Wild West figure named John Wesley Hardin, who shot and killed a sheriff. While in prison, Hardin studied law and was released early. He began to practice his new trade in El Paso, Texas, but just a year later he was killed by a law officer.

With the Vietnam War more divisive than ever, a new kind of hero began to emerge among young people: the anti-hero. These were people who did good but rebelled against authority or sometimes broke the law to do so. Many who felt the Vietnam War was immoral burned their draft cards in public and refused to be inducted into the armed service. They were anti-heroes—those

Bob Dylan in 1966, at the Mayfair Hotel in London. Even though he was not in the public eye, he continued to write and perform music and to find new inspiration.

who broke the law to do what they thought was right. In a similar manner, John Wesley Hardin was an anti-hero.

Dylan's hero, Woody Guthrie, died in 1967, and several musicians planned a memorial concert. Dylan came out of his retreat to perform three songs with the Band. The next year he released another album, *Nashville Skyline*, which received mixed reviews but sold well. He also appeared at a huge music festival on the Isle of Wight, in Great Britain.

The next year, 1970, he released two more albums. One, *Self Portrait*, was a two-record set and was disliked by most critics and fans. The next, *New Morning*, was better received. In September, Dylan left his country home and moved back to Greenwich Village in New York City. With many singers and celebrities there, Dylan would not stand out as he did in small Woodstock.

Dylan turned thirty in 1971 and celebrated his birthday quietly in Tel Aviv, Israel, with his family. He appeared to be getting in touch with his religion, which he had mostly ignored since his childhood. Dylan prayed at the Western Wall, the only remaining remnant of the second temple in Jerusalem and dating to the year 70. It is the holiest site in Judaism. Dylan said, "I'm a Jew. It touches my poetry, my life, in ways I can't describe."[7]

"Doin' God's Work"

. . . .

Bob Dylan, actor? Why not? The Beatles and Elvis Presley basically played fictional versions of themselves in their movies. Dylan wasn't going to do something that easy. A movie director named Sam Peckinpah felt Dylan was a good choice to appear in his next film, *Pat Garrett and Billy the Kid*. It was based on a true story of two outlaws who were friends in the Old West. Billy the Kid, whose real name was William Bonney, murdered twenty-one men and lacked respect for human life. His friend Pat Garrett became a sheriff and was ordered to find and capture Billy, dead or alive.

The movie was released in the summer of 1973 to mixed reviews. Some said it was slow moving while others felt it was a strong character study. Dylan also composed the movie soundtrack, which was released as an album and reached number 12 on the national album chart.[1] One cut, a haunting ballad titled "Knockin' on Heaven's Door," was released as a 45 and went to number

Bob Dylan tried his hand at movie acting, taking on the role of a character named Alias in the 1973 movie *Pat Garrett and Billy the Kid.*

• •

12.[2] Although the soundtrack was a hit with the public, many critics panned it. Vincent Canby of the the *New York Times* wrote, "The music is so oppressive that when it stops we feel giddy with relief, as if a tooth had suddenly stopped aching."[3]

With his debut acting job behind him, Dylan embarked on his first tour since the motorcycle accident. He played forty shows from early January through mid-February 1973.

Things were going well in the mid-1970s. Bob and Sara got busy building a mansion on their California property, and Dylan also bought a farm near Minneapolis,

Minnesota, to use as a retreat. He was less angry with the press but still avoided dealing with them whenever possible. Dylan also began to play up the importance of religion in his life. In an interview he said, "I don't care what people expect of me. Doesn't concern me. I'm doin' God's work. That's all I know."[4]

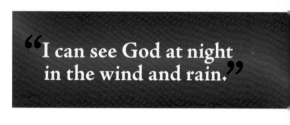

"I can see God at night in the wind and rain."

In another one, he was asked how he imagines God. Dylan declared, "I can see God in a daisy. I can see God at night in the wind and rain. I see creation just about everywhere."[5]

Tapes from the Basement

Anything with Bob Dylan's name on it seemed to turn to gold. The tapes Dylan had privately made with the Band in Woodstock in 1967 had been released illegally over the previous several years. Illegal recordings are called bootlegs. They become available when someone obtains copies of the original recordings and makes and sells their own copies. It is against the law since the recording artist receives nothing for his or her work. Dylan and Columbia Records decided they might as well make an official recording of those tapes.

A total of twenty-four songs from the sessions were released in July 1975 on a two-album set titled *The Basement Tapes*. Critics raved, calling the release one of Dylan's best. While it did not sell as well as Dylan's newest material, *The Basement Tapes* was a hit nonetheless, reaching number 7 on the national album chart.[6]

The Winds of Hibbing

A lot of Bob Dylan's early songs mention the wind. There is a good reason why. When he was a kid, one of the most popular places he and his friends rode their bicycles to was the Hull-Rust open pit iron mine. It is said to be the largest such pit mine in the world. And one can't help but feel the winds while standing on a modest hilltop overlooking it. Several Dylan songs mention the wind. Perhaps the best known are "Blowing in the Wind," "Girl from the North Country," and "Subterranean Homesick Blues."

Although *Planet Waves* and *Blood on the Tracks* were heavy with personal songs about relationships, Dylan did not give up political activism. An advertising executive named George Lois had gotten wind of a true story of what appeared to be an example of failed justice.

Professional middleweight boxer Rubin "Hurricane" Carter and a man named John Artis were convicted of murdering three white men in a Paterson, New Jersey, bar in 1966. Carter and Artis, both African Americans, insisted they were innocent. They claimed they had been framed by dishonest white police officers and a racist court system. Then in 1974, two witnesses admitted lying under oath. The case was officially reopened and Carter and Artis were given new trials.

Carter was no angel. He had a strong temper and had been convicted of crimes such as petty theft. In a 1964 magazine, Carter was quoted as saying white police officers should be killed. He later explained that his words had been taken out of context. Still, George Lois believed Carter did not commit murder and began championing the fighter's cause. Lois sent a copy of Carter's autobiography, *The Sixteenth Round*, to celebrities including Dylan. Dylan was so touched by the book that he visited Carter in prison.

Convinced that Carter had been framed, Dylan and a cowriter named Jacques Levy composed a song telling Carter's version of the case. The song, "Hurricane," appeared on Dylan's next album, *Desire*, and was also released as a 45. It made the top forty, but was often played on FM stations, which at the time generally did not play pop 45s. George Lois played a tape of the song to Carter while visiting him in prison. Lois recalled, "He lost his mind! It was beautiful. There was (sic) tears in his eyes. He was crying."[7]

Rolling Thunder

Meanwhile, Dylan busily organized his next tour. It would be something new—a sort of cross between a rock concert and alternative theater. Dylan called it the Rolling Thunder Revue. Dylan would play small-town theaters and auditoriums as well as massive arenas. While he would have regular backup musicians, the tour was open to well-known entertainers who felt like dropping by to share the stage. At one stop in Toronto, even Dylan's mother, Beatty, made an appearance.

Dylan usually went onstage wearing a fedora hat, faded jeans, and a black vest over a white shirt. Some nights his face was painted white. Critics and fans analyzed what kind of statement he was trying to make by appearing in whiteface. Was he making a comment on some kind of injustice in society? Dylan gave what some said to be a misleading answer: he just wanted people in the back rows to be able to see his face. A performer with the Rolling Thunder Revue, singer and actress Ronee Blakley, summed up the tour's electric atmosphere. "It was like the circus came to town," she announced.[8]

Two concerts, in New York City and Houston, were designated as benefits to help pay for a new trial

A benefit concert for boxer Hurricane Carter featuring Bob Dylan and the Rolling Thunder Revue took place in New York City in 1975. The concert's proceeds helped to fund Carter's legal costs.

for Hurricane Carter, now out on bail. At the New York concert, celebrated heavyweight boxing champ Muhammad Ali pleaded with the audience to get involved in Carter's cause. In March, Carter's and Artis's convictions were thrown out by a New Jersey court that ruled that they did not get a fair trial.

Renaldo and Clara

To top things off, Dylan decided to have the concert tour taped. He wanted to make a movie including tour scenes. It would be somewhat different from his earlier concert tour movie, *Don't Look Back*. This would have concert scenes but also include rehearsed dialogue and a plot. Dylan's wife, Sara, would have a starring role in this film to be called *Renaldo and Clara*.

Who were Renaldo and Clara? True to type, Dylan answered evasively. To one reporter he announced, "Renaldo is a fox and Clara is supposedly the clear understanding of the future which doesn't exist."[9] Who could even figure out what that meant?

About this time Bob and Sara Dylan's marriage was starting to fall apart. They argued about all sorts of things ranging from Dylan's rock-and-roll lifestyle to how their California mansion should be designed. There were rumors that Dylan was having extramarital relationships with women in his show and that he had returned to smoking and drug use.

In late fall, Hurricane Carter was again put on trial. The happiness of Dylan and other Carter supporters turned to dismay as the witnesses changed their stories once more and said they told the full truth in the

One of the Best Concert Films Ever

Dylan was part of another concert film in 1976. The Band was splitting up and arranged a farewell show in San Francisco. As a tribute to his friends, Dylan announced he would join them for four songs. Since he did not want this concert movie to compete with *Renaldo and Clara*, Dylan allowed director Martin Scorsese to film him singing only two songs. The film was titled *The Last Waltz* and is regarded by numerous critics as one of the best concert films ever made.

first trial. Carter and Artis were found guilty again in December 1976 and resentenced to life in prison.

Meanwhile, on March 1, 1977, Sara Dylan filed for divorce. A court gave Sara custody of the children, and she moved the family from Malibu to Beverly Hills, where the children attended school.

The praise afforded to *The Last Waltz* was not given to *Renaldo and Clara*. Dylan's movie premiered in New York and Los Angeles on January 25, 1978. Nearly every critic hated it. For one thing, the movie was nearly four hours long. Some felt it was hard to follow. The *New York Times* gave it one of its better reviews, though it was not a glowing one. It said, "The film contains more than its share of dead weight, but it is seldom genuinely dull."[10]

Dylan had spent $1.25 million of his own money making *Renaldo and Clara*. It earned very little in return.[11] Meanwhile, he had many bills to pay for both the construction of his mansion and the lawyers handling his divorce. To earn money, he embarked on a lengthy world tour in February 1978, which took him to four continents. While on tour, he had a romantic relationship with a backup singer named Helena Springs. He soon began seeing Mary Alice Artes and Carolyn Dennis. All three were African American women with strong links to Christianity. A very controversial period of Dylan's life was about to begin.

CHAPTER EIGHT

Faith and Feeding the Hungry

. . . .

Mary Alice Artes introduced Bob Dylan to the ministers at her church, the Vineyard Fellowship. The evangelical church's religious philosophy is the total opposite of the political and religious views Dylan had always held. Evangelical Christians believe in the Bible as the literal word of God. They also strongly feel that only people who accept Jesus as their savior get to Heaven. Their views on moral issues are very conservative. But Dylan was taken with the church's spiritual leaders. Before long he was regularly attending Bible classes and services at the Vineyard Fellowship. Dylan was soon baptized and officially admitted into the Christian faith.

Dylan said that although Artes had led him to the fellowship, it was a personal and mystical experience with Jesus that made him a Christian. He recalled a morning in his Malibu house when he stated, "There was a presence in the room that couldn't have been anybody but Jesus. I truly had a born-again experience, if you want to call it that. It was a physical thing. I felt it all over me. I felt my whole body tremble."[1]

Early in 1979, Dylan began recording a new album titled *Slow Train Coming*, with songs reflective of his newfound Christian faith. A single from the album, "Gotta Serve Somebody," became a top forty hit, reaching number 24 in the fall of 1979.[2] The album was even bigger, reaching number 3 on the national album chart.[3]

> "I truly had a born-again experience, if you want to call it that."

Christianity took over Dylan's life. When he went on tour to promote his new album, he and his musicians prayed before each performance. One night he did not think he would be able to sing since he had a sore throat. His singers prayed for him before the show. Dylan seemed to recover and did his show as usual.

Even though *Slow Train Coming* sold well, not all accepted the new religious Bob Dylan. The majority of his longtime fans could not stand to hear Dylan preaching through his music. He was booed at nearly every concert he played that year.

Dylan's family and Jewish friends found the legendary singer's conversion to Christianity insulting. They felt he had become a traitor to his faith. Dylan said he had expected angry reactions. "Not surprised at all," he answered when asked about them. He played up the minority who accepted his new music. "I'm just surprised to hear applause every time I play. I appreciate that. You can feel everything that comes off an audience

The late 1970s were a controversial time in Bob Dylan's career. His music during this time reflected his exploration into Christianity, causing some to question his authenticity.

. . . little individual things that are going on. It's a very instant thing."[4]

His next album, *Saved*, released in June 1980, included more original songs about Christian beliefs. It did not sell nearly as well as *Slow Train Coming*, reaching 24 on the national album chart. While *Slow Train Coming* stayed on the chart twenty-six weeks, *Saved* lasted only eleven. It was his worst charting album since *Another Side of Bob Dylan* in 1964.[5]

Doubters

Some fans and critics did not believe Dylan was a true Christian. They theorized that he felt empty and depressed following his divorce and grabbed on to the first new idea he came across. Others said he turned to Christianity only to please his girlfriend. Still others insisted Dylan was recording Christian music only to make money. The Born-Again Christian movement was growing in the United States. US president Jimmy Carter was a born-again Christian. Keith Richards of the Rolling Stones said Dylan was merely a "prophet of profit."[6]

Despite such talk, Dylan seemed sincere. He stated publicly, "What Jesus does for an ignorant man like myself is to make the qualities and characteristics of God more believable to me, cos I can't beat the devil. Only God can."[7]

Regardless of his newfound faith, the next several months were troubling ones. A fan named Carmel Hubbell became obsessed with Dylan. She insisted she had once been Dylan's girlfriend and began referring to herself as Carmel Dylan. Hubbell constantly phoned Dylan and his staff and followed him to theaters where he performed.

Then on December 8, 1980, a tragic event occurred when a crazed fan shot and killed John Lennon of the Beatles. Dylan panicked that there would be copy-cat attacks on other musicians. He sent security people in advance to check the concert halls where he was to play and went so far as to buy one of his backup musicians a bullet-proof vest.[8]

With fear for his safety in the back of his mind, Dylan tried carrying on. Carmel Hubbell did not make it easy. In June 1981, she barged into the studio where he was recording, only to be forced out by Dylan's staff. She then moved into an apartment close to Dylan's California home and began leaving threatening notes. At Dylan's urging, a court served Hubbell a restraining order, forcing her by law to stay away from the singer.

Dylan's third and last Christian-themed album, *Shot of Love*, came out in September 1981. It was a bit of a departure from *Slow Train Coming* and *Saved* in that it included nonreligious songs. Like *Saved*, it did not sell well, reaching number 33 on the national album chart and staying for a measly nine weeks.[9] But with secular songs on the album, it appeared Dylan was going back to his old form.

Those who followed Dylan's life noted that he seemed to be returning to his Jewish roots. In 1982, he celebrated his son Samuel's bar mitzvah. Then in the fall of 1983, Dylan's son Jesse had his bar mitzvah in Jerusalem at the Western Wall. Jesse was in his mid-teens by then, but he had not had a bar mitzvah at age thirteen as is customary. A widely circulated photograph showed the proud father wearing the skullcap and prayer shawl worn during prayer by traditional Jews.

Back in the United States, Dylan spent much time with a group of ultra-religious Orthodox Jews called Chabad Lubavitch. In addition, his next album, *Infidels*, included a song he wrote called "Neighborhood Bully," which was interpreted as a defense of Israel in its longtime struggle with its Arab neighbors.

What did Dylan have to say about all this? As usual, nothing clear. To one reporter Dylan confessed that he had had no problem with his Christian preaching. But he added, "maybe the time for me to say that has come and

Chabad Lubavitch

Chabad Lubavitch is a movement of Orthodox Jews. Among the most conservative philosophies of Judaism it takes the Bible literally as the word of God. While Chabad Lubavitch followers live according to strict religious rules, they are also known for their humanitarian work. They actively provide meals, medical care, and shelter to victims of natural disasters and terror attacks. In addition, the movement also offers programs for special needs children and maintains a rehabilitation center in Los Angeles for people with substance abuse problems. Generally, they provide aid to people regardless of their personal religious faith.

gone. It's time for me to do something else. Sometimes those things appear quickly and disappear. Jesus himself only preached for three years."[10]

Out of Seclusion

The legend began to come out of seclusion in March 1984, singing three songs on the television show *Late Night with David Letterman*. He followed with a lengthy tour of Europe, in which he appeared with Joan Baez again for two concerts in Germany.

A tragedy half a world away brought some of the world's best-known musicians together in an unlikely event. As a result of a civil war raging in the African nation of Ethiopia, millions there were starving to death. Bob Geldof, a member of Irish rock group the Boomtown Rats, came up with a novel way to raise money. Late in 1984, he gathered together some of England's best-known bands to record a song titled, "Do They Know It's Christmas?" It is still played on radio stations every December. Money from record sales went to Ethiopian famine relief.

American musicians thought it was a wonderful idea and decided to record a similar song. In January 1985, Dylan and forty-five other artists recorded "We Are the World." Included with Dylan were some of music's hottest names including Bruce Springsteen, Stevie Wonder, Diana Ross, Billy Joel, and Michael Jackson. This multitude of musicians was called USA for Africa. "USA" had a double meaning, standing for the United States of America and also for United Support of Artists. "We Are the World" was massive, reaching number one and staying at the top of the charts for four weeks that spring.[11]

Bob Geldof got together with two concert promoters to take this unusual charity event to the next level. On July 13, 1985, two rock concerts took place at the same time—one in London, the other in Philadelphia. Together, the twin concerts were known as Live Aid. Live Aid was televised for sixteen hours and featured rock's greatest artists. Phil Collins pulled off a tough feat: he played drums at the London concert, then flew a

Bob Dylan (*left*) performed with Keith Richards at Philadelphia's Live Aid in 1985. Although their performance was poorly received, the twin concerts brought in $50 million for famine relief.

The Grammy Awards

In February 1980, Bob Dylan won his first Grammy Award. The Grammys are given to members of the recording industry for excellence in recorded media. While most know the Grammys for awarding music honors, they also recognize spoken word and comedy recordings. For decades, music critics faulted the Grammys for ignoring rock and roll at the expense of middle-of-the-road music. Now, they were finally recognizing rock music with its own categories. Dylan won his award for his single "Gotta Serve Somebody," in the category of Best Male Rock Vocal Performance.

Concorde airplane across the Atlantic to play drums the same day in Philadelphia.

Dylan was given a position of honor, the last solo act in the Philadelphia show. He rendered old classics including "Blowin' in the Wind," accompanied by Keith Richards and Ron Wood of the Rolling Stones. Unfortunately, the sound equipment was not set up well and the quality was poor. But Live Aid was more about famine relief than a big party. The two concerts raised some $50 million to feed the starving.[12]

As might be expected, Dylan stirred up a bit of controversy. During his set, he suggested using some of the money raised during Live Aid to help American farmers. There was an economic crisis at the time affecting farmers in the United States. Many with farms in their families for generations could not afford to keep them. Dylan, being from a small Minnesota town and owner of his own farm, understood their problems.

Though Dylan's heart may have been in the right place, concert officials thought he stepped out of line. Americans might have been losing their farms, but Africans were starving to death. Dylan seemed insensitive to the purpose of Live Aid.

Dylan's speech helped propel another charity concert to take place, however. Popular country music singer Willie Nelson took Dylan's idea and ran with it. Nelson organized Farm Aid, with the purpose of helping American farmers pay off huge debts to keep

From left to right, guitar pioneer Les Paul, British musician Dave Edmunds, and Bob Dylan rock the house at the 1988 Rock and Roll Hall of Fame induction concert in New York City.

their farms. The Farm Aid concert took place amid the soybean fields of Champaign, Illinois, on September 22, 1985. Dylan, Nelson, and other rock and country entertainers including Johnny Cash, Waylon Jennings, and Neil Young performed.

Dylan was as busy as ever. He released four albums in 1985 and 1986, including a five-record volume of fifty-three songs, including eighteen new ones. He also had a wedding in his future. Sometime-girlfriend Carolyn Dennis had become pregnant with his child. Their daughter, Desiree Gabrielle Dennis-Dylan, was born on January 31, 1986. Dylan secretly married Dennis on the following June 4. The marriage was kept private, and this time word was not leaked to the media.

For the next few years, Dylan actively wrote songs, released albums, and performed live. He also made another movie, called *Hearts of Fire*, in which he played a fictional music performer named Billy Parker. However, the movie was a disaster. It was first released in England, where it received poor reviews and played for only a few weeks. It was never released in the United States. Then on January 20, 1988, Bob Dylan received what to many rockers is the ultimate honor—he was inducted into the Rock and Roll Hall of Fame.

Elder Statesman

· ·

W hen Dylan was inducted into the Rock and Roll
Hall of Fame many fans felt he was past his prime.
His concerts drew diehards but did not fill stadiums. He
seemed to have to share the bill with another big act to
sell out a stadium. But Dylan always seemed to have
something new in the works. If he didn't embark on a
project on his own, someone would contact him. That
is exactly what happened in the early spring of 1988.
Former Beatle George Harrison was in Los Angeles to
make a quick record. Jeff Lynne, the project's producer,
had once played guitar and keyboards with British
band Electric Light Orchestra (ELO). Harrison and
Lynne were looking for an inexpensive studio. Harrison
recalled, "And the only studio we could find available
was Bob's. So we thought Bob's got one, we'll just call
him up."[1]

Lynne was also producing records for Tom Petty
and Roy Orbison, one of rock music's pioneers who had

several hits in the early 1960s. Petty and Orbison were invited to come along for the recording session. The talented quintet began jamming and writing new songs and decided to make them into an album. They called their impromptu group the Traveling Wilburys. Orbison said, "We all enjoyed it so much. It was so relaxed. There was no ego involved and there was some sort of chemistry going on."[2]

Supergroup the Traveling Wilburys was born almost by accident. Counterclockwise from top left are Jeff Lynne, Dylan, Tom Petty, George Harrison, and Roy Orbison. The band recorded two albums.

It was a time of personal changes for Dylan. In April 1989, he and Carolyn bought a new home. This was not in a glamorous town such as Malibu or Beverly Hills, but a Los

> "There was no ego involved and there was some sort of chemistry going on."

Angeles suburb called Tarzana. No one would have expected to find Bob Dylan there, and he was determined to keep his and his family's privacy.

He appeared to be returning even more strongly to his Jewish roots by appearing at a Los Angeles fund-raiser for Chabad Lubavitch. At the event, Dylan played the Jewish folk tune "Hava Nagila." Then on November 7, 1989, he became a grandfather for the first time. His stepdaughter Maria and her husband, Peter, had a son they named Isaac.

A New Hit Album

There was another new addition to Dylan's legacy that fall. The album *Traveling Wilburys Volume 1* was released and reached number three on the national album chart, higher than any solo Dylan album since *Slow Train Coming* nine years earlier.[3] Sadly, Roy Orbison did not live to see its success. He died of a heart attack on December 6, 1988, at age fifty-two. Dylan, Lynne, Petty, and Harrison released a second Traveling Wilburys album in October 1990. Although it was the group's second album, they jokingly titled it, *Traveling Wilburys Volume 3*, and it reached number 11.[4]

An Inspiring Memory

In January and February of 1959, a rock concert tour was hitting the towns of the upper Midwest. It was called Winter Dance Party. One of the stars was rock legend Buddy Holly. Dylan saw the concert on January 31 in Duluth. On February 3, Holly, rock novelty rocker the Big Bopper and Mexican American singer Ritchie Valens died in a small airplane crash just after takeoff following a performance. Dylan referred to the concert while accepting his Grammy Award for *Time Out of Mind*. "When I was about 16 or 17 years old, I went to hear Buddy Holly play at the Duluth National Guard Armory, and I was three feet away from him, and he looked at me and … I know he was with us all the time when we were making this record in some kind of way."[5]

In the fall of 1990, the United States was on the brink of war against Iraq and there was a surge of patriotism in the country. The nation's mood was the polar opposite of the disruptive days of the Vietnam War. Whether it was intentional or not, in October Dylan played his first concert in a military setting. The venue was the United States Military Academy at West Point, New York. Who would have thought Bob Dylan, once so antimilitary and antiwar, would be entertaining army cadets?

On the verge of turning fifty, Dylan had become a senior statesman of rock music. The Grammy Awards honored him with a Lifetime Achievement Award on February 20, 1991. While accepting the honor, Dylan gave a bizarre speech. Standing at the podium, he looked ill. Some said Dylan had the flu. Others have maintained he was drunk while once again abusing alcohol. On national television, Dylan stated, "Well, my daddy, he didn't leave me much, you know he was a very simple man, but what he did tell me was this, he did say, 'son,' he said."

Dylan then paused for a long time, as if he forgot what he wanted to say. Uneasiness filled the hall. Some in the audience laughed nervously.

Dylan and movie legend Jack Nicholson share a laugh onstage at the 33rd annual Grammy Awards ceremony in New York City in 1991. Dylan received a Lifetime Achievement Award that night.

Dylan finished his thoughts, continuing, "he say, 'you know it's possible to become so defiled in this world that your own father and mother will abandon you and if that happens, God will always believe in your ability to mend your ways.'"[6]

Biblical experts recognized that Dylan's words were based on a verse from the Bible. Psalms, chapter 27, verse 10, reads: "For though my father and mother have forsaken me, The Lord will take me up."[7] It is recited by Jews during prayer services in the month before the Jewish New Year.

Dylan fans have since analyzed just what he meant that night. Did his father really say those words or did Dylan just make that up? Did he plan to say them that night or did the words just come out on the spur of the moment? And who was he referring to about becoming "defiled"? The music industry? People in general? Somebody specific in his life?

One Dylan biographer, Howard Sounes, wrote, "It seemed to many watching that Bob was talking about himself, meaning that his father would have been shocked by the state he was in if he could have been there to see him."[8]

To his fans, all that mattered was the man's music. A total of fifty-eight previously unreleased Dylan songs were packaged as *The Bootleg Series, Volumes 1–3* and released in March 1991. They sold moderately well and were highly thought of by critics. The next year, Dylan marked three decades in the recording industry with a gala Thirtieth Anniversary Celebration concert in New York City's Madison Square Garden.

Soon afterwards, Dylan and his second wife, Carolyn, divorced. With Dylan on the road so often, they were rarely together. Their divorce took place as secretly as their wedding had.

Although no longer a chart topper, Dylan was invited to perform at high-profile events. In January 1993, he sang at the Lincoln Memorial as part of President Bill Clinton's first inauguration gala. In the summer of 1994 he finally performed at Woodstock. This was Woodstock '94, a concert celebrating the twenty-fifth anniversary of the groundbreaking first Woodstock concert that Dylan had snubbed.

Dylan on MTV

In the fall of 1994, Dylan showed that while he might be middle-aged, he was no rock-and-roll dinosaur. Music video cable network MTV invited him to sing as part of its "Unplugged" series, where well-known music artists performed acoustically. On December 14, Dylan sang most of his classics, and the concert was released as both a compact disc (CD) and videotape. It was one of his highest-ranking albums in years, peaking at number 23 the following spring.[9]

It was also in the mid-1990s that some observers say that Dylan started taking better care of himself. However, Dylan denied having any alcohol problem. When told that some writers said he was drinking too much, Dylan responded, "That's completely inaccurate."[10] He explained his opinion of those writers. "They might hear rumors. They might start rumors, but it's their own minds going to work."[11]

Regardless, it was clear that Dylan was morphing from one of rock's elder statesmen into a living legend. If an ambassador of rock music was needed, Dylan was called upon. This included some unlikely events, such as the eightieth birthday of Frank Sinatra.

Known as "the Chairman of the Board," Sinatra, like Dylan, was a music legend. But he was from a different age, having become popular in the early 1940s during the big band era. To rock-and-roll fans, Sinatra represented their parents' tastes. Yet here they were together in 1995—Bob Dylan and Frank Sinatra, two music greats from different generations, side by side.

Then Dylan's name was raised in a place that years earlier would have been unheard of. A college professor named Gordon Ball, who taught English and fine arts at the Virginia Military Institute (VMI), nominated Dylan for the Nobel Prize for Literature. Ball wrote to the Nobel Academy, "Since the early 1960s Mr. Dylan in word and music has created an almost unlimited universe of art which has permeated the globe and in fact changed the history of the world."[12] Dylan did not win the singular honor, but the fact that he was nominated and taken seriously proved his acceptance by the mainstream.

Dylan turned fifty-six in 1997, and his daughter Maria arranged a small birthday party for the family. At the party, Maria noticed her father did not look well. A doctor diagnosed him with a condition called pericarditis, the result of a fungal infection. The condition caused a sac around his heart to inflame, and it could have been very serious, possibly fatal. Luckily, it was treated in time, and Dylan was released from the hospital six days later.

He joked about his brush with death, saying, "I really thought I'd be seeing Elvis soon."[13]

Though still weak and sometimes dizzy from his illness, Dylan worked on a new album, *Time Out of Mind*. He also toured that summer and in September played for one of his most distinguished audiences. At an important religious meeting in Bologna, Italy, Dylan played for two hundred thousand fans including Pope John Paul

I really thought I'd be seeing Elvis soon.

II. The pope sat to the side as Dylan sang several numbers including "Knockin' on Heaven's Door." After the set, the pope referred to Dylan in a sermon. The seventy-seven-year-old pope said to the young audience, "Just before, a representative of yours said on your behalf that the answer is blowing in the wind. Yes. It is true ... on the wind that is the voice and breath of the Spirit."[14] The honors kept coming. On December 7, 1997, Bob Dylan received the esteemed Kennedy Center Medal. President Clinton presided over the ceremony, and Dylan brought his eighty-two-year-old mother to sit by his side. It was probably the first time people saw Bob Dylan wearing a tuxedo.

Ten years earlier it appeared that Dylan would be one of those rock artists whose best days were in the past. But *Time Out of Mind* became Dylan's best-selling album since *Slow Train Coming*. It reached number 10 on the national album chart and stayed in the top one hundred for twenty-nine weeks.[15] At the Grammy Awards in

February 1998, it won in three categories including "Album of the Year."

Bob Dylan was still very relevant. In 2000, *Hurricane*, a feature film based on Hurricane Carter's life and starring Denzel Washington, drew many to the theaters. Included on the soundtrack was Dylan's 1975 song "Hurricane." Then in 2001, Dylan won his first Academy Award, given by the movie industry, for his song "Things Have Changed." It was on the soundtrack of a movie called *The Wonder Boys*. And in May that year, online voters in Great Britain voted him the greatest lyricist of

Jakob Dylan

Bob Dylan's children successfully managed to stay out of the public eye. The exception was son Jakob. In the early 1990s he formed a band called the Wallflowers. Their first album bombed, but their second album, called *Bringing Down The Horse,* released in 1997, was a mega-hit. To Jakob's credit, he did not take advantage of his family name. He was just one member of the band. On November 17, both the Wallflowers and Dylan were in San Jose, California, and father and son performed on the same bill. While Bob was winning awards at the 1998 Grammy celebration, the Wallflowers also won two awards for "One Headlight," their hit single from *Bringing Down the Horse.*

A reporter covering the event for the *New York Times* wrote, "at the 40th annual Grammy Awards ceremony, the Dylan name was a guaranteed winner."[16]

all time. He gathered 32.6 percent of the total vote. John Lennon was second with 18 percent.[17]

Return to Newport

Even though Dylan was about to turn sixty, he was not free from controversy. In 2001, Dylan biographer Howard Sounes announced the news that Dylan had been able to keep quiet for so long—that he was secretly married to Carolyn Dennis. Earlier books had always referred to Dennis as Dylan's girlfriend. Dennis confirmed publicly that Sounes was correct and declared, "Bob and I made a choice to keep our marriage a private matter for a simple reason—to give our daughter a normal childhood."[18]

On February 27, 2002, Dylan won another Grammy Award. It was in the category of Best Contemporary Folk Album for *Love and Theft*. Then on August 3, he performed at the Newport Folk Festival for the first time since his legendary appearance in 1965. Under a fake wig and white cowboy hat and behind a false beard, Dylan rendered new numbers such as "Cry Awhile" and classics including "The Times They Are A-Changin'" and "Like a Rolling Stone." He performed both acoustically and electrically, and while there was no controversy this time, the Newport homecoming received mixed and poor reviews.

Dylan never stopped being busy. He wrote his first autobiography, which was published in 2004. After his hit album *Modern Times* was released in 2006, he went on to release five more studio albums and four live ones. The song styles on *Modern Times* included blues, rockabilly, and balladry. Almost all music critics praised the album. *Rolling Stone* magazine declared it the absolute best album of 2006.[19]

The aging troubadour was the subject of two more documentaries, one released in 2005, the other in 2007. And in 2006, he decided he'd tackle a completely new project. He hosted a weekly radio show called *Theme Time Radio Hour*. It was broadcast on XM Satellite Radio. The show was a rambling mixture of early country and blues from the 1930s, new wave bands from the late 1970s and early 1980s, and even some hip-hop. He filled some of the breaks between songs by telling stories. He even took the liberty of reading a critical fan letter while on the air. Someone sent Dylan an email asking, "What do you have against new songs?" Dylan had a simple explanation. "The truth is there's a lot more old songs than there are new songs."[20]

New Names for Minnesota Streets

By now, the folks in Hibbing who once resented Dylan began to appreciate the brilliant performer who grew up in their town. The street where Dylan lived, 7th Avenue East, was changed to Bob Dylan Drive in the mid-2000s. Duluth residents had the same idea. In 2006 they renamed a 1.8-mile stretch in downtown Bob Dylan Way.

In 2009, Dylan stunned critics and fans—something he had plenty of practice doing—by releasing an album of traditional Christmas songs, both modern secular and old religious ones. The record included "Silver Bells," "The First Noel," "Hark The Herald Angels Sing," and "Must Be Santa." The compact disc cover art was a vintage lithograph from the nineteenth century. He said

Bob Dylan continues to receive honors for his illustrious career. President Barack Obama presented him with the Presidential Medal of Freedom in 2012. It is the nation's highest civilian honor.

· · · · · · · · · · · · · · · · · · · ·

that being Jewish had nothing to do with the album's release. The Christmas songs are, he said, "part of my life, just like folk songs."[21] Dylan gave all the profits from the album to charities fighting hunger and homelessness.

Well into his seventies, Dylan was hardly done with shocking people. His long-time fans wondered what he must have been thinking when they saw him in television ads for Pepsi and Cadilllac. Why was he hawking products? Here was one of counterculture's royalty appearing in ads for products made by the biggest corporations in the world.

What topped that was another ad with Bob Dylan representing a mega-corporation. In October 2016, during a broadcast of *Monday Night Football*, suddenly Dylan was having a conversation with a computer named Watson in a commercial for IBM. IBM is known for being a very conservative business. Typically, Dylan was silent.

But Dylan has always been an enigma. And now he finally was honored with the Nobel Prize for Literature he was nominated for years earlier. What can he do to top that? We'll have to wait and see.

Chronology

1941 Robert Allen Zimmerman is born in Duluth, Minnesota, on May 24.

1947 Moves with family to Hibbing, Minnesota.

1955 Sees movie *Rebel Without a Cause,* which deeply influences him.

1958 Stirs up controversy with wild performance at high school talent show.

1959 Graduates high school.

1959 Attends University of Minnesota.

Around 1960 Changes stage name to Bob Dylan.

1960 Moves to Denver, Colorado.

Around late 1960–early 1961 Moves to New York City.

1961 Meets and befriends idol Woody Guthrie; first rave review in the *New York Times* on September 29; signs first recording contract with Columbia Records on October 26.

1962 First album, *Bob Dylan,* is released on March 19; legally changes name to "Bob Dylan" on August 9.

1963 Becomes hero to young people when he turns down chance to appear on national television over censorship issue; second album, *The Freewheelin' Bob Dylan,* released on May 27 and becomes first hit on national chart; first plays Carnegie Hall.

1964 Third album, *The Times They Are A-Changin'*, released in February; fourth album, *Another Side of Bob Dylan* is released in August.

1965 Fifth album, *Bringing It All back Home*, is released in March; controversial appearance at Newport Folk Festival on July 25; single "Like A Rolling Stone" hits number 2; sixth album, *Highway 61 Revisited*, released in August; secretly marries Sara Lownds on November 22.

1966 Son Jesse is born on January 6; moves to Woodstock, New York, in May; seventh album, the classic *Blonde on Blonde*, released in May; motorcycle accident in July spurs semiretirement.

1967 Privately records *The Basement Tapes* with members of the Band June–October; daughter Anna is born July 11.

1968 *John Wesley Harding* is released in January; son Samuel is born July 30.

1969 *Nashville Skyline* released in April; plays Isle of Wight Festival August 31; son Jakob is born December 9.

1970 *Self Portrait* and *New Morning* are released; moves back to New York City.

1971 Celebrates thirtieth birthday in Israel; plays Bangladesh benefit concert.

1973 Movie *Pat Garrett and Billy the Kid* and soundtrack album are released; first concert tour since motorcycle accident.

1974 *Planet Waves* becomes Dylan's first number one album.

1975 *The Basement Tapes* is released in July; single "Hurricane" is released in fall.

1975 Tours with Rolling Thunder Revue.

1977 Files for divorce from Sara on March 1.

1978 Movie *Renaldo and Clara* is released January 25; begins long world tour.

1979 Release of *Slow Train Coming* in August signals Dylan's conversion to Christianity.

1980 Wins first Grammy Award for "Gotta Serve Somebody."

1983 Releases *Infidels*, first album without Christian theme since *Slow Train Coming*; spends time with Orthodox Jewish religious group Chabad Lubavitch.

1985 Sings on "We Are the World"; plays Live Aid July 13; plays Farm Aid November 22.

1986 Daughter Desiree Gabrielle Dennis-Dylan is born on January 31; Dylan secretly marries Desiree's mother Carolyn Dennis on June 4.

1988 Inducted into Rock and Roll Hall of Fame.

1989 Album *Traveling Wilburys Volume I* is released and is a huge hit

1991 Receives Lifetime Achievement Grammy Award at age forty-nine; *The Bootleg Series Volumes 1–3* released in March; secretly divorces second wife, Carolyn.

1993 Performs at President Bill Clinton's inaugural ceremony.

1995 Album *MTV Unplugged* released.

1996 First nominated for Nobel Prize for Literature.

1997 Hospitalized with fungal infection; plays for Pope John Paul II in Italy; album *Time Out of Mind* is released; receives Kennedy Center honor on December 7.

1998 *Time Out of Mind* sweeps Grammy Awards.

2000 Feature film *Hurricane* is released, which includes Dylan's 1975 song of same name on soundtrack.

2001 Song "Things Have Changed" earns Dylan's his first Academy Award.

2002 Plays Newport Folk Festival for the first time since controversial 1965 appearance.

2005 Martin Scorcese's documentary about Bob Dylan, *No Direction Home*, is broadcast on PBS's *American Masters* series.

2006 Releases hit album, *Modern Times*; hosts weekly radio show.

2009 Releases Christmas album with all profits going to charity.

2016 Wins Nobel Prize for Literature.

Selected Discography

Bob Dylan (Columbia, 1962)

The Freewheelin' Bob Dylan (Columbia, 1963)

The Times They Are A-Changing' (Columbia, 1964)

Another Side of Bob Dylan (Columbia, 1964)

Bringing It All Back Home (Columbia, 1965)

Highway 61 Revisited (Columbia, 1965)

Blonde on Blonde (Columbia, 1966)

Bob Dylan's Greatest Hits (Columbia, 1967)

John Wesley Harding (Columbia, 1968)

Nashville Skyline (Columbia, 1969)

Self Portrait (Columbia, 1970)

New Morning (Columbia, 1970)

Bob Dylan's Greatest Hits, Vol. II (Columbia, 1971)

Pat Garrett & Billy the Kid (Columbia, 1973)

Planet Waves (credited to Bob Dylan and the Band) (Asylum, 1974)

Before the Flood (credited to Bob Dylan and the Band) (Asylum, 1974)

Blood on the Tracks (Columbia, 1975)

The Basement Tapes (credited to Bob Dylan and the Band) (Columbia, 1975)

Desire (Columbia, 1976)

Slow Train Coming (Columbia, 1979)

Saved (Columbia, 1980)

Shot of Love (Columbia, 1981)

Infidels (Columbia, 1983)

Empire Burlesque (Columbia, 1985)

Biograph (Columbia, 1985)

Traveling Wilburys, Vol. 1 (credited to the Traveling Wilburys) (Wilbury, 1988)

Dylan & the Dead (credited to Bob Dylan and the Grateful Dead) (Columbia, 1989)

The Bootleg Series—Volumes 1–3 (Columbia, 1991)

Traveling Wilburys, Vol. 3 (credited to the Traveling Wilburys) (Wilbury, 1990)

Good as I Been to You (Columbia, 1992)

World Gone Wrong (Columbia, 1993)

Greatest Hits Volume 3 (Columbia, 1994)

MTV Unplugged (Columbia, 1995)

Time Out of Mind (Columbia, 1997)

The Bootleg Series Vol. 4—Live 1966 (Columbia, 1998)

The Essential Bob Dylan (Columbia, 2000)

Love and Theft (Columbia, 2001)

Modern Times (Columbia, 2006)

Together Through Life (Columbia, 2009)

Christmas in the Heart (Columbia, 2009)

Tempest (Columbia, 2012)

Shadows in the Night (Columbia, 2015)

Fallen Angels (Columbia, 2016)

Triplicate (Columbia, 2017)

Chapter Notes

Introduction

1. Laura Smith-Spark, "Bob Dylan Wins 2016 Nobel Prize for Literature, CNN, October 13, 2016, http://edition.cnn.com/2016/10/13/world/nobel-prize-literature/.

2. Ibid.

3. Ben Sisario, Alexandra Alter, and Sewell Chan, "Bob Dylan Wins Nobel Prize, Redefining Boundaries of Literature," *New York Times*, October 13, 2016. https://www.nytimes.com/2016/10/14/arts/music/bob-dylan-nobel-prize-literature.html?_r=1.

4. Edna Gunderson, "World Exclusive: Bob Dylan— I'll be at the Nobel prize ceremony… if I can," *London Telegraph*, October 29, 2016, http://www.telegraph.co.uk/men/the-filter/world-exclusive-bob-dylan---ill-be-at-the-nobel-prize-ceremony-i/.

5. Ibid.

6. "Bob Dylan—Banquet Speech," Nobelprize.org, December 10, 2016, http://www.nobelprize.org/nobel_prizes/literature/laureates/2016/dylan-speech_en.html.

Chapter 1: Radio Stations from Far Away

1. Clinton Heylin, *Bob Dylan: Behind the Shades Revisited* (New York, NY: William Morrow, 2001), p. 7.

2. Robert Shelton, *No Direction Home: The Life and Music of Bob Dylan, July 3–9, 1978* (New York, NY: Beech Tree Books, 1986), p. 30.

3. Shelton, pp. 30–31.

4. "The Philippe Adler Interview: July 1978." http://www.interferenza.com/bcs/interw/78-jul.htm.

5. Shelton, p. 34.

6. Shelton, p. 35.

7. Johnny Ray home page, http://www.johnnyray.com.

8. Bob Spitz, *Dylan: A Biography* (New York, NY: Viking Penguin, Inc., 1989), p. 33.

Chapter 2: Next Stop Greenwich Village

1. Robert Shelton, *No Direction Home: The Life and Music of Bob Dylan* (New York, NY: Beech Tree Books, 1986), p. 47.

2. Bob Spitz, *Dylan: A Biography* (New York, NY: Viking Penguin, Inc., 1989), p. 61.

3. Ibid.

4. Editors of *Memories* magazine, *Yearbook* (New York, NY: Dolphin, Doubleday, 1990), p. 107.

5. "The Philippe Adler Interview: July 1978." http://www.interferenza.com/bcs/interw/78-jul.htm.

6. "Playboy Interview: Bob Dylan." http://www.interferenza.com/bcs/interw/66-jan.htm.

7. Tim Riley, *Hard Rain: A Dylan Commentary* (New York, NY: Alfred A. Knopf, 1992), pp. 18–19.

8. Nat Hentoff, "The Crackin', Shakin', Breakin' Sounds," *New Yorker*, October 24, 1964. http://www.newyorker.com/magazine/1964/10/24/the-crackin-shakin-breakin-sounds.

9. Shelton, *No Direction Home*, p. 65.

Chapter 3: "Goin' t'see Woody"

1. Bob Spitz, *Dylan: A Biography* (New York, NY: Viking Penguin, Inc., 1989), p. 113.

2. Tim Riley, *Hard Rain: A Dylan Commentary* (New York, NY: Alfred A. Knopf, 1992), p. 18.

3. Spitz, p. 114.

4. Spitz, p. 153.

Chapter 4: John Hammond Takes a Chance

1. "October 1961, Billy James Interview, New York City, New York." http://youngbutdailygrowin.com/wip/interviews/610929.01.html.

2. Ibid.

3. Bob Spitz, *Dylan: A Biography* (New York, NY: Viking Penguin, Inc., 1989), p. 193.

4. Ibid.

5. Clinton Heylin, *Bob Dylan: Behind the Shades Revisited* (New York, NY: William Morrow, 2001), p. 116.

6. Joel Whitburn, *The Billboard Book of Top 40 Hits* (New York, NY: Billboard Publications, Inc., 1996), p. 468.

7. Ibid.

8. "'I Am My Words,'" *Newsweek*, November 4, 1963, p. 94.

9. Ibid., pp. 94–95.

10. Robert Shelton, *No Direction Home: The Life and Music of Bob Dylan* (New York, NY: Beech Tree Books, 1986), p. 246.

11. Patrick Humphries and John Bauldie, *Absolutely Dylan: An Illustrated Biography* (New York, NY: Viking Studio Books, 1991), p. 178.

Chapter 5: What Really Happened at the Newport Folk Festival?

1. Clinton Heylin, *Behind the Shades Revisited: Bob Dylan* (New York, NY: William Morrow, 2001), p. 165.

2. David Hajdu, *Positively 4th Street: The Lives and Times of Joan Baez, Bob Dylan, Mimi Baez Farina and Richard Farina* (New York, NY: Farrar, Straus & Giroux, 2001), p. 203.

3. Joel Whitburn, *The Billboard Book of Top 40 Hits* (New York, NY: Billboard Publications, Inc., 1996), p. 196.

4. Robert Shelton, *No Direction Home: The Life and Music of Bob Dylan* (New York, NY: Beech Tree Books, 1986), p. 300.

5. Dave Marsh, "Out of the 60's, Into His 50's," May 19, 1991, http://www.nytimes.com/books/97/05/04/reviews/dylan-50.html.

6. Whitburn, p. 196.

7. Shelton, p. 279.

8. Hajdu, p. 260.

9. Jac Holzman, "Stuff You Don't Know About the 60s," "Dylan Goes Electric at Newport 1965," http://www.followthemusic.com/chapter-seven/.

10. Hadju, pp. 260–261.

11. Richie Unterberger, *Turn! Turn! Turn! The '60s Folk-rock Revolution* (San Francisco, CA: Backbeat Books, 2002), p. 19.

12. Thomas Meehan, "Public Writer No. 1?," *New York Times*, December 12, 1965, http://www.nytimes.com/books/97/05/04/reviews/dylan-writer.html.

13. Ibid.

14. Whitburn, p. 95.

15. Ibid., p. 620.

16. Ibid., p.119.

17. Ibid., p. 235.

Chapter 6: Major Changes

1. Robert Shelton, "Dylan Conquers Unruly Audience," *New York Times*, August 30, 1965, p. 20.

2. Ibid.

3. Personal interview with Mary Keyes, July 28, 2014.

4. Joel Whitburn, *The Billboard Book of Top 40 Hits*, (New York, NY: Billboard Publications, Inc., 1996), p. 196.

5. Patrick Humphries and John Bauldie, *Absolutely Dylan: An Illustrated Biography* (New York, NY: Viking Studio Books, 1991), p. 199.

6. Jann S. Wenner, "Bob Dylan Talks: A Raw and Extensive First Rolling Stone Interview," *Rolling Stone*, November 29, 1969. http://www.rollingstone.com/music/news/bob-dylan-talks-a-raw-and-extensive-first-rolling-stone-interview-19691129.

7. Robert Shelton, *No Direction Home: The Life and Music of Bob Dylan* (New York, NY: Beech Tree Books, 1986), p. 300.

Chapter 7: "Doin' God's Work"

1. Joel Whitburn, *Joel Whitburn's Top Pop Albums* (Menominee Falls, WI: Record Research, Inc., 2001), p. 255.

2. Joel Whitburn, *The Billboard Book of Top 40 Hits* (New York: Billboard Publications, Inc., 1996), p. 196.

3. Vincent Canby, "Screen: Peckinpah's 'Pat Garrett and Billy the Kid,'" *New York Times*, May 24, 1973, p. 53.

4. Jim Jerome, "Bob Dylan: A Myth Materializes with a New Protest Record and a New Tour," *People*, November 10, 1975, http://www.interferenza.com/bcs/interw/75-nov10.htm.

5. Neil Hickey, profile of Bob Dylan, *TV Guide*, September 11, 1976. http://www.interferenza.com/bcs/interw/76-sep11.htm.

6. Joel Whitburn, *Joel Whitburn's Top Pop Albums,* p. 255.

7. Howard Sounes, *Down the Highway: The Life of Bob Dylan* (New York, NY: Grove Press, 2001), p. 292.

8. Sounes, p. 294.

9. "The Karen Hughes Interview in Sydney April 1, 1978," *Rock Express No. 4.* http://www.interferenza. com/bcs/interw/78-apr1.htm.

10. Janet Maslin, "'Renaldo and Clara,' Film by Bob Dylan," *New York Times,* January 26, 1978, p. C18.

11. Sounes, p. 314.

Chapter 8: Faith and Feeding the Hungry

1. Larry Yudelson, "Dylan: Tangled Up in Jews," 1991, *Washington Jewish Week.* http://www.radiohazak.com/ Tangled.html.

2. Joel Whitburn, *The Billboard Book of Top 40 Hits* (New York, NY: Billboard Publications, Inc., 1996), p. 196.

3. Joel Whitburn, *Joel Whitburn's Top Pop Albums* (Menominee Falls, WI: Record Research, Inc., 2001), p. 255.

4. Henry Tiernan, "The Diamond Voice Within," *New Musical Express*, August 15, 1981, pp. 29–31.

5. Joel Whitburn, *Joel Whitburn's Top Pop Albums*, p. 255.

6. Howard Sounes, *Down the Highway: The Life of Bob Dylan* (New York, NY: Grove Press, 2001), p. 335.

7. Tiernan.

8. Sounes, pp. 337–338.

9. Joel Whitburn, *Joel Whitburn's Top Pop Albums*, p. 255.

10. Robert Shelton, *No Direction Home: The Life and Music of Bob Dylan* (New York, NY: Beech Tree Books, 1986), p. 488.

11. Joel Whitburn, *The Billboard Book of Top 40 Hits*, p. 625.

12. Shelton, p. 494.

Chapter 9: Elder Statesman

1. Elliot J. Hutley, *Mystical One: George Harrison* (Toronto, Canada: Guernica Editions, 2004), p. 219.

2. Ibid.

3. Joel Whitburn, *Joel Whitburn's Top Pop Albums,* (Menominee Falls, WI: Record Research, Inc., 2001), p. 892.

4. Ibid.

5. Jon Pareles, "Dylans, Father and Son, Gather Grammies; Shawn Colvin Wins for 'Sunny,'" *New York Times,* February 26, 1998, p. B9.

6. Ronnie Schreiber, "Dylan's Grammy Acceptance Speech Explicated." http://www.radiohazak.com/ Dylgramm.html.

7. *The Holy Scriptures,* (Philadelphia, PA: The Jewish Publication Society of America, 1955), p. 883.

8. Howard Sounes, *Down the Highway: The Life of Bob Dylan* (New York, NY: Grove Press, 2001), p. 395.

9. Joel Whitburn, *Joel Whitburn's Top Pop Albums,* p. 256.

10. Mikal Gilmore, "Bob Dylan," *Rolling Stone,* November 22, 2001, Gilmore, p. 64.

11. Ibid.

12. "Bob Dylan—Finally and Formally Launched as a Candidate for the Nobel Prize for Literature, 1997," press release. http://www.expectingrain.com/dok/art/ nobel/Nobelpress.html.

13. "Bob Dylan Released from Hospital Treatment Continues and Full Recovery Expected," Sony Music press release, June 2, 1997. http://www.edlis.org/twice/threads/dylan_hospitalization_update.html.

14. Andrea Orlandi, "The Show 27/9." http://www.interferenza.com/bcs/itpope.htm.

15. Joel Whitburn, *Joel Whitburn's Top Pop Albums,* p. 246.

16. Jon Pareles, "Dylans, Father and Son, Gather Grammies; Shawn Colvin Wins for 'Sunny', *New York Times,* February 26, 1998, p. B9.

17. "Dylan 'The Greatest Songwriter', May 23, 2001. http://news.bbc.co.uk/hi/english/entertainment/music/newsid_1347000/1347071.stm.

18. "Dylan's Game of Hide and Seek," ABC News, April 12, 2001. http://abcnews.go.com/Entertainment/story?id=106870.

19. Rollingstone.com, "Albums of the Year and End of the Year Critic Lists," April 20, 207. http://www.rocklistmusic.co.uk/rolling.htm#2006.

20. Miranda Sawyer, "The Great Sound of Radio Bob," *Guardian*, December 30, 2006. https://www.theguardian.com/media/2006/dec/31/observerreview.radio.

21. *International Busines Times*, "Bob Dylan Brings Christmas Cheer to Those Without Homes," November 26, 2009. http://www.ibtimes.com/bob-dylan-brings-christmas-cheer-those-without-homes-187008.

Glossary

A&R Short for artists and repertoire, the division of a record label that scouts talent and develops recording artists.

acoustic Without electronic amplification.

beatnik Subculture during the 1950s and 1960s representing the Beat generation.

bootleg Illegal music recording, often made at a concert.

Chabad Lubavitch Conservative Jewish movement or philosophy.

cinema verite Realistic and natural style of documentary filmmaking.

elder statesman Well-respected and experienced person in a field.

eponymous Named after a person.

evangelical Following the teaching of the Christian gospel.

folk music Music that is often not written down but passed down orally; often serves as protest music.

45 A single on a vinyl recording that plays at 45 rotations per minute (RPM).

Grammy Award Award given by members of the recording industry for excellence in recorded media.

jazz Musical genre developed in the early twentieth century by African Americans that relies on improvisation.

LSD An illegal chemical compound that causes people to hallucinate, or see and perceive things that are not there.

Nobel Prize Esteemed award given annually in the fields of literature, physics, chemistry, medicine, economics, and peace.

press The manufacturing of vinyl records.

rhythm and blues A genre originating with African American musicians that served as a precursor to rock and roll.

satire A literary genre that uses humor to expose a weakness or negativity.

secular Having no connection to religion.

Further Reading

Books

Bell, Ian. *Once Upon a Time: The Lives of Bob Dylan.* New York, NY: Pegasus Books, 2014.

Brown, Donald. *Bob Dylan: American Troubadour.* Lanham, MD: Rowman & Littlefield, 2016.

Dylan, Bob. *The Lyrics: 1961–2012.* New York, NY: Simon & Schuster, 2016.

Robertson Robbie, Jim Guerinot, Sebastian Robinson, and Jared Levine. *Legends, Icons & Rebels: Music That Changed the World.* Toronto, Ontario: Tundra Books, 2016.

Websites

Bob Dylan.com
www.bobdylan.com
Bob Dylan's official website.

Rock and Roll Hall of Fame
www.rockhall.com
Located in Cleveland, Ohio, the Rock and Roll Hall of Fame offers exhibits and concerts.

Bob Dylan's Facebook Page

www.facebook.com/bobdylan/
Dylan's Facebook page offers current information on the musician.

Films

Bob Dylan: 30th Anniversary Concert Celebration, dir. Gavin Taylor (1993).

Bob Dylan: Don't Look Back, dir. D.A. Pennebaker (1967).

Index

Rock and Roll Hall of
Fame, 90–91
Rolling Stones, 83, 88
Rolling Thunder Revue,
75–76
Rothchild, Paul, 59, 59
Rotolo, Suze, 37, 43, 45,
47–48, 49
Rubin, Judy, 21, 25, 27–28

S
Sigma Alpha Mu, 24–24
Sinatra, Frank, 98
Springs, Helen, 79
Standard Oil Company,
8–9, 11
St. Paul, Minnesota, 24,
25–26, 28

T
Thomas, Dylan, 27
Traveling Wilburys, 92, 93

U
University of Minnesota,
24–25

V
Van Ronk, Dave, 42

Vietnam War, 65, 68, 94
Vincent, Gene, 23

W

Washington Square Park,
34, 35, 42
"We Are the World," 86–87
Whitaker, David, 28
Williams, Hank, 14–16, 43
WMFG radio station,
14, 17
Woodstock, NY, 65–66, 70
Woodstock festival, 66, 97
Woodstock festival
(1994), 87
Workman, David Tice, 17

Z
Zimmerman, Abram
(father), 8–9, 11–12,
22, 47
Zimmerman, Beatrice
("Beatty"; mother), 9,
10–11, 12, 13, 47, 75, 99
Zimmerman, David
Benjamin (brother),
11, 21